SAP Certified Application Associate – Financial Accounting (FI) with SAP ERP 6.0

By

K. Kiran & Augustine D.

Copyright Notice

Table of Contents

Before you Start..

Before you start here are some Key features of the SAP Financial Accounting (FI) Associate Certification Exam.

- The certification test "Application Associate - Financial Accounting (FI) with SAP ERP 6.0 " verifies proven skills and fundamental knowledge in the area of the SAP Financial Accounting.
- It proves that the candidate has a good overall understanding within this consultant profile and can implement this knowledge practically in projects under guidance of an experienced consultant.
- The exam is Computer based and you have three Hours to answer 80 Questions.
- The Questions are (mostly) multiple choice type and there is NO penalty for an incorrect answer.
- Some of the Questions have more than one correct answer. You must get ALL the options correct for you to be awarded points.
- For questions with a single answer, the answers will have a button next to them. You will be able to select only one button.
- For questions with multiple answers, the answers will have a 'tick box' next to them. This allows you to select multiple answers.
- You are not allowed to use any reference materials during the certification test (no access to online documentation or to any SAP system).
- The Official Pass percentage is 65%. (This can vary slightly for your exam)
- In this book, unless otherwise stated, there is only one correct answer.

A Quick Quiz

Q 1. The organizational units of Financial Accounting are used for external reporting purposes, that is, they fulfil requirements that your business is subject to from external parties, for example, legal regulations.
Which of the following Organizational units are mandatory in an ERP system with FI?
(More than one answer is correct)

A. Client
B. Business Area
C. Company code
D. Company

Answer:
A, C

You create your company-specific organizational structure in the SAP System by defining the organizational units and making the basic settings. Defining organizational units for Financial Accounting is obligatory, that is, you have to define these units in order to be able to implement the Financial Accounting component.

Organizational unit	Definition
Client	*Obligatory*
Company	Optional
Company code	*Obligatory*
Business area	Optional

Apart from this, there are certain Basic settings that are mandatory as well. These are:
Chart of accounts, Fiscal year, Currencies

Q 2. You can configure different types of Chart of Accounts in the ERP system. Some of these are:
(More than one answer is correct)

A. Operating chart of accounts
B. Group chart of accounts
C. Country-specific chart of accounts
D. Plant specific chart of accounts

Answer:
A, B, C

Charts of accounts can have three different functions in the system:

- **Operating chart of accounts**

The operating chart of accounts contains the G/L accounts that you use for posting in your company code during daily activities. Financial Accounting and Controlling both use this chart of accounts.
You have to assign an operating chart of accounts to a company code.

- **Group chart of accounts**

The group chart of accounts contains the G/L accounts that are used by the entire corporate group. This allows the company to provide reports for the entire corporate group.
The assigning of an corporate group chart of accounts to a company code is optional.

- **Country-specific chart of accounts**

The country-specific chart of accounts contains the G/L accounts needed to meet the country's legal requirements. This allows you to provide statements for the country's legal requirements.
The assigning of an country-specific chart of accounts to a company code is optional.

Q 3. The company code, business area and controlling area organizational units can be combined in a number of ways. Using these combinations you can represent organizations with different structures. Which of the following are valid combinations?
(More than one answer is correct)

A. One Company Code can be assigned to multiple Controlling areas
B. One Controlling area can be assigned to multiple company codes
C. One business area can be assigned to multiple company codes
D. One company code can be assigned to multiple business areas

Answer:
B, C, D

- One Controlling Area is Assigned to One Company Code

In this example, the financial accounting and cost accounting views of the organization are identical.

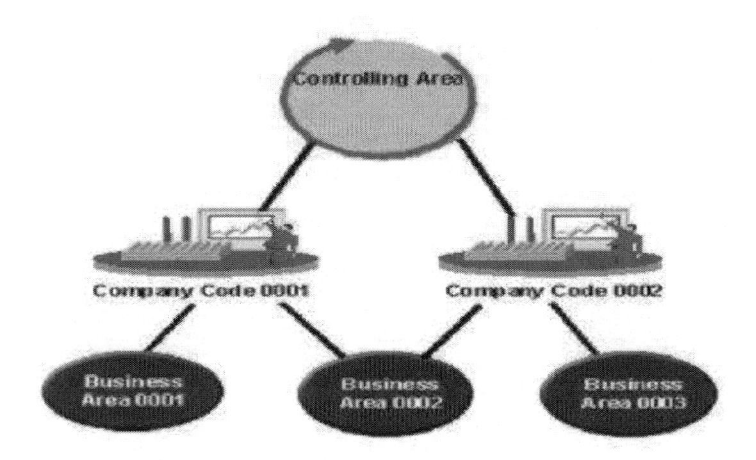

- Multiple Company Codes Assigned to One Controlling Area

This example is Cross-Company Code Cost Accounting. Cost accounting is carried out in multiple company codes in one controlling area. All cost-accounting relevant data is collected in one controlling area and can be used for allocations and evaluations. In this case, the external and internal accounting perspectives differ from each other. For example, this method can be used if the organization contains a number of independent subsidiaries using global managerial accounting. Cross-company code cost accounting gives you the advantage of using internal allocations across company code boundaries.

Company Codes and Business areas have an **n:m** relationship

Q 4. You need to assign more than one company code to one controlling area. Under what kind of a business scenario would you need to consider such a decision? (More than one answer is correct)

A. Cross-company code transactions that MUST be processed in a controlling area
B. Multilevel Product Cost Management across company codes
C. Representation of intercompany processes, whereby producing and delivering plant are the same.

Answer:
A, B

A **1:n relationship** between controlling area and company code is recommended for the following situations:

- Cross-company code transactions that MUST be processed in a controlling area, for example, production in an associate plant, special cases of intercompany processing.

- Cross-company code CO postings that can be displayed in the reconciliation ledger, such as assessments, capitalization of internal activity in Asset Accounting, activity allocation.

- Representation of group costing.

- Use of Profit Center Accounting and transfer prices.

- Multilevel Product Cost Management across company codes

A **1:1 relationship** between controlling area and company code is recommended for the following situations:

- Consolidated analysis of settled transactions across company codes in Profitability Analysis (CO-PA) In this situation, you assign more than one controlling area to an operating concern

- Representation of intercompany processes, whereby producing and delivering plant are the same.

Q 5. Which of the following tax types does the SAP System support for calculating, posting, and correcting tax, as well as for tax reporting?

A. Tax on sales & purchases
B. Withholding Tax
C. Top Up Tax
D. Additional Tax

Answer:
A, B, D

The following Tax types are supported in a standard SAP system:

Tax on sales and purchases
Taxes on sales and purchases are levied on every sales transaction in accordance with the principles of VAT. This applies to input and output tax, for example.
Input tax is calculated using the net invoice amount and is charged by the vendor.
Output tax is calculated using the net price of products and is charged to the customer.
Companies can offset input tax against output tax, paying the balance to the tax

authorities. Tax authorities can set a nondeductible portion for input tax which cannot then be claimed from the tax authorities.

Additional tax

Additional taxes are taxes that are posted in addition to tax on sales/purchases. They are usually country-specific, such as investment tax in Norway, or sales equalization tax in Belgium.

Sales tax

An example of sales tax is the sales and use tax that exists in the USA. Sales transactions that are taxed must be kept strictly separate from sales transactions that are not taxed.
In general, goods that are intended for production or for resale to a third party are procured untaxed; that is, the vendor does not calculate tax on the sale of these goods (sales tax). Procurement transactions for individual consumption, on the other hand, are taxable (use tax).
The principle of sales tax does not permit the option of offsetting input tax against output tax. The vendor must pay the taxes to the tax authorities.
The system calculates sales tax based on material and customer location and posts it in Sales and Distribution (SD) and Materials Management (MM). If customers or vendors are exempt from taxation, you can specify this in their master records by entering the appropriate indicator.

Withholding tax

In some countries, a portion of the invoice amount must be withheld for certain vendors and paid or reported directly to the tax authorities.
SAP currently provides two functions for calculating withholding tax: Classic withholding tax and extended withholding tax.

Extended withholding tax includes all the features of classic withholding tax and, in addition, also fulfills a number of further country-specific requirements.
If you wish to implement the withholding tax functions, you should choose extended withholding tax.

Q 6. Depending on your system's configuration, the system can generate and post line items automatically. For which business transactions can this be done?
(More than one answer is correct)

A. Entering a customer invoice
B. Entering Special G/L transactions
C. Posting a Vendor Payment

Answer:
A, B, C

The following line items are generated for each of the above business transactions:

Entering a customer or vendor invoice

- Tax on sales/purchases (output tax when posting a customer invoice, input tax when posting a vendor invoice)
- Payables and receivables between company codes (when posting cross-company code transactions)

Posting a customer or vendor payment and clearing open items

- Cash discount (paid and received when posting payments)
- Backdated tax calculation for tax on sales/purchases (after cash discount deduction)
- Gains and losses from exchange rate differences (between invoice and payment)
- Unauthorized deduction of cash discount (when a payment is slightly different to the amount due)
- Residual items
- Bank charges

Entering special G/L transactions

- Bill of exchange charges
- Tax adjustment for a down payment

Q 7. You can add details to any automatically generated line item. For example, you can add text to a tax on sales/purchases line item.

A. True
B. False

Answer:
A

If you are permitted to make additional account assignments to the automatically generated line items, the system branches directly to the document overview. Here, the automatically generated items are highlighted.

To enable this, you need to make sure that the G/L account is marked as adjustable and that the appropriate field is defined as optional or required in the field status group.

Q 8. The document type is a key that is used to classify accounting documents. It is entered in the document header and applies to the whole document.
Which of the following purposes are achieved by using document types?
(More than one answer is correct)

A. Assigning document numbers
B. Posting to account types
C. Clearing line items
D. Differentiating between business transactions

Answer:
A, B, D

The following purposes are served by using 'Document Types:

- **Differentiating between business transactions**. The document type tells you instantly what sort of business transaction is in question. This is useful, for example, when displaying line items for an account.

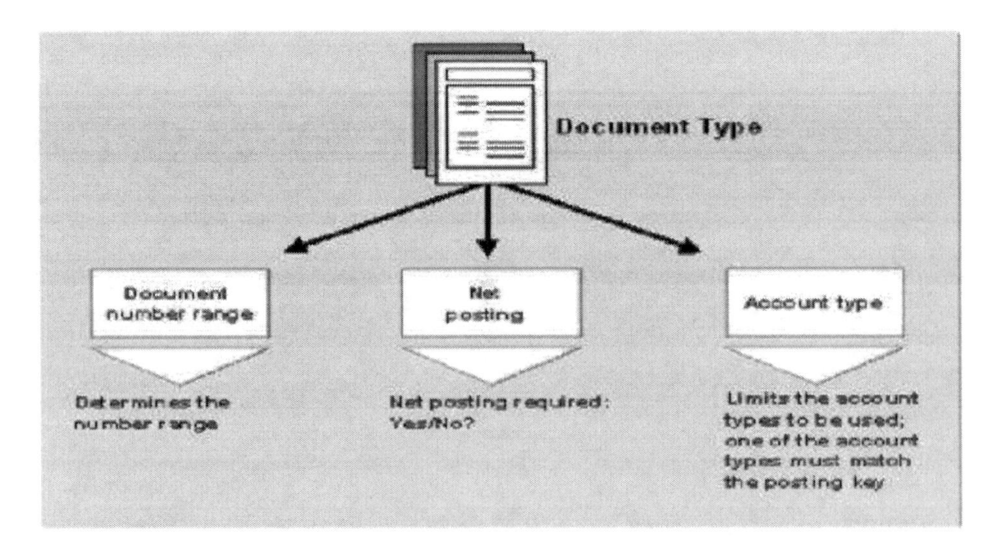

- **Controlling the posting to account types (vendor, customer, or G/L**

accounts). The document type determines which account types that particular document can be posted to.

- **Assigning document numbers.** A number range is assigned to every document type. The numbers for the documents you create are taken from this number range. The original documents from one number range should be stored together. In this way, the document type controls document storage.
For more information, see Document Number Assignment and Controlling Document Storage Using the Document Type

- **Applying the vendor net procedure.** This means that any discount and the net amount are calculated (and posted) when the vendor invoice is posted.

Q 9. If you have entered an incorrect document, you can reverse it, thereby also clearing the open items. With reference to 'document reversal', which of the following are true?
(More than one answer is correct)

A. A document can be reversed if it has no cleared items
B. Documents in MM can be reversed with a credit memo
C. If the posting period of the source document has already been closed, you have to enter a date that falls in an open posting period (for example, the current one) in the Posting date field.

Answer:
A, C

A document can only be reversed if:

- It contains no cleared items
- It contains only customer, vendor, and G/L account items
- It was posted with Financial Accounting
- All entered values (such as business area, cost center, and tax code) are still valid

If a line item from a source document has been cleared, a reversal can only be carried out after the clearing is reset. Information on clearing is available in FI General Ledger Accounting as well as FI Accounts Receivable and Accounts Payable.

Documents from SD can be reversed with a credit memo.

Documents from MM must be reversed with functions in that component because the reversal function in FI does not reverse all the values required.

There are two ways of updating transaction figures when reversing a document:

- The document and the reverse document increase the account transaction debit and credit figures by the same amount.
- After a document has been reversed, the balance of the account affected is

shown as if the document had never been posted. (Negative Postings)

You generally post the reversal document in the same posting period as the corresponding original document. If the posting period of the source document has already been closed, you have to enter a date that falls in an open posting period (for example, the current one) in the Posting date field.

Q 10. A number of periodic tasks are executed on a regular basis (daily, weekly, or monthly) in the SAP System. This process is supported by the individual components of the Schedule Manager. Which of the following are components of the Schedule Manager?
(More than one answer is correct)

A. Flow definition
B. Scheduler
C. Monitor
D. Exception area

Answer:
A, B, C

The following are the key components of schedule manager:

Flow definition
In a flow definition, you can link tasks to each other if they are related or if you wish to use a worklist in them. You can therefore schedule a flow definition as a task in the scheduler.

Scheduler

In the scheduler, you can schedule tasks in a structure tree. You can use drag-and-drop in a daily overview to enable the system to execute the tasks at a certain time.

Monitor

The monitor gives you an overview of the scheduled tasks during and after processing.
You can correct faulty objects in a worklist.

Worklist

Objects that are to be processed in a processing step sequence are managed in the worklist.
The worklist monitor presents information such as which objects were processed without errors and which objects could not be processed. You can display information on the cause of errors, and thus control the way in which the object is processed further.
The worklist ensures that when a processing step sequence is processed again, the system only processes the objects which had errors or which you manually instructed the system to reprocess.

Q 11. You would like to use recurring entries for periodic transaction. Which of the following are False with reference to 'recurring entries'?

A. Posting Key, Account and Amount never change in recurring entries
B. Postings can be made periodically or on a specific date
C. Recurring documents do Not require a separate number range.

Answer:
C
Recurring entries are business transactions that are repeated regularly, such as rent or insurance. The following data never changes in recurring entries:

- Posting key
- Account
- Amounts

You enter this recurring data in a recurring entry original document. This document does not update the transaction figures. The recurring entry program uses it as a basis for creating accounting documents.
Structure
The system uses the recurring entry original document that you enter as a reference. It is not an accounting document and therefore does not affect the account balance. In the recurring entry document, you define when a posting is to be created with this document. You have two options for scheduling. Postings can be made periodically or on a specific date:

- For periodic postings, specify the first and last day of execution, as well as the interval in months.
- If you want to specify certain dates, enter a run schedule in the recurring entry original document. Store the required dates in the Implementation Guide (IMG).

Choose Financial Accounting Global Settings → Document → Recurring Entries → Define Run Schedules/Enter Run Dates.

To post recurring entry documents, you have to set up a separate number range for the company codes that use them. You have to use key X1 for the number range. The system takes numbers for the recurring entry original document from this number range.

Q 12. You are responsible for 'dunning' configuration. Which of the following are part of configuring the dunning functionality?

A. Dunning Codes
B. Dunning Items
C. Dunning areas

Answer:
C

The dunning configuration consists of configuring the following:

- **Dunning procedure**

The dunning procedure controls how dunning is carried out by the system. You can define as many dunning procedures as you like.

- **Dunning level**

The dunning levels are calculated based on the number of days open items are in arrears.
You can also have the system calculate the dunning levels based on the dunning amount or a percentage paid (sales-related dunning level determination).
You can determine more than one dunning level per dunning procedure.

- **Dunning areas**

A dunning area is an organizational unit within a company code used for the dunning process.
A dunning area can be a division or a sales organization. You assign a dunning area to an open item when you are posting. You can dun items separately by dunning area.

Fundamentals/Master Date (FI/CO)

1) Which of the statements on document principles are correct?

a) Each business event creates an accounting document in R/3
b) A business event might trigger more than one document in R/3.
c) R/3 will link related documents in the system

(More than one answer correct)

Answer – b, c

Explanation:

Not every business event creates an accounting document in R3. Raising a purchase order creates a document in the MM module but does not generate an accounting document. Accounting entries are only generated when a purchase order is converted to a goods receiving note.

A business event may trigger more than one document. Converting a goods receipt to an invoice verification, for example, will generate three documents respectively: a materials document, an accounting document, and a profit center document. R3 will link related documents in the system. The source document can be seen from the accounting document.

2) Which of the following statements are true

a) The G/L account name for house bank must match the names given to the house bank in the bank directory
b) The G/L account names for house banks are user-definable
c) The G/L account names for house banks could be the bank name and account number
d) The G/L account names for house banks are defined in bank directory

e) At company code level, G/L account names for house banks can be different from those in chart of accounts

(More than one answer correct)

Answer – b, c

Explanation:

GL account description and the house bank name in the bank directory can either be the same or it can have different names.

Each bank account is represented in the SAP ERP system by a combination of house bank ID and account ID. This combination is entered in a G/L account that represents the bank account in the general ledger.

You must also define bank accounts that are managed at the house banks. The accounts can be identified by an account ID that is unique for each house bank.

The bank account data contains the number of the account at your bank, the account currency, and the relevant G/L account.

A G/L account must be created for each bank account. This G/L account is assigned to the bank account and vice versa. Both accounts must have the same account currency.

House banks are defined at the client level and not at the company code level

3) Which prerequisites are checked by the system before deleting master data?

a) For GL account: has a deletion indicator been set?
b) For customers: have they been created before 1995
c) For vendors: are there still transaction figures?
d) For GL accounts, customers and vendors: are there still documents?
e) For banks: is a bank balance sheet overdrawn?
f) For banks: are they still being used?

(More than one answer is correct)

Answer – a, c, d, f

Explanation:

You can mark a customer master record for deletion using the deletion indicator. If for example, you no longer maintain business relationships with the customer. The master record is only deleted after all dependent data has been deleted. Furthermore, you can only delete master data in Financial Accounting if no transactions have been posted to the corresponding accounts.

4) Where do you define the reconciliation account that will be used by an asset?

a) Account determination in asset class
b) Account number in fixed asset
c) Account determination in depreciation area
d) Account number in depreciation area

(Only one answer correct)

Answer - c

Explanation:

Reconciliation accounts for each asset class will be defined in the account determination for the depreciation area. The asset cost account, accumulated depreciation and the depreciation accounts are some of the accounts which are specified in this area.

5) The depreciation position program RAPOST2000 can be used to record the following:

a) Ordinary (book and cost accounting) depreciation
b) Tax special depreciation or the allocation and write off of reserves for special depreciation on the basis of tax special depreciation
c) Unplanned depreciation (or other manually planned depreciation)
d) Imputed interest
e) APC revaluation below/above the accumulated depreciation

(More than one answer is correct)

Answer – a, b, c, d, e

Explanation:

You can post the following using the depreciation posting program RAPOST2000:

- Ordinary depreciation (book depreciation and cost-accounting)
- Tax depreciation, or allocation and write-off of reserves due to special tax

- Depreciation
- Unplanned depreciation (or other manually planned depreciation)
- Imputed interest
- Revaluation of APC or of accumulated depreciation

6) The 'posting period' can be defined for each

a) Company code
b) Accounting principle
c) Posting period variant
d) Accrual type

(More than one answer is correct)

Answer – a, b, d

Explanation:

The posting period is defined for each company code, accounting principle and the accrual type.

7) The 'purpose of account determination' is to determine the following:

a) Document type
b) Debit account
c) Credit account
d) Balance sheet account

(More than one answer is correct)

Answer – a, b, c

Explanation:

The purpose of account determination is to
- Determine the document type
- Determine the debit account (here: target account)
- Determine the credit account (here: start account)

For each accrual type, you define in Customizing which postings are to be made automatically and, therefore, for which postings account determination is required.

8) Which of the following are fields of 'General Data' in customer/vendor accounts?

a) Address
b) Insurance
c) Control data
d) Account management

(More than one answer is correct)

Answer – A, C

Explanation:

Insurance and the account management is maintained at the company code level. Additional fields also can be added through a coding block in SAP.

9) In SAP every document is uniquely identified by the following fields.

a) Company code
b) Document number
c) Fiscal year
d) Posting period

(More than one answer is correct)

Answer – a, b, c

Explanation:

Each document in SAP can be uniquely identified by the company code, document number and the fiscal year combination. At the beginning of the financial year the document number ranges need to be created.

10) Consider the following statements:

1. **Secondary cost elements area used in production that are produced from outside the company.**
2. **Cost elements are indicators, used as a basis for allocations and for performing key figure analysis.**
3. **Cost centers are the organizational units that incur and influence costs.**

Which of the above sentences is true (Please choose the correct option)?

a) 1
b) 2
c) 3
d) all of them
e) none of them

(Only one answer is correct)

Answer – c

Explanation:

Cost centers are separate areas within a controlling area at which costs are incurred. You can create cost centers according to various criteria including functional considerations, allocation criteria, activities provided, or according to their physical location and/or management area.
Secondary cost elements are used to allocate overheads but not the direct production costs.
Cost elements can be used to allocate costs but key figure analysis is carried out by using statistical key figures.

11) During a fiscal year, you can only change the assignments of the organizational units company code, business area or profit center to a cost center if:

1. **The currency of the new company code is the same as the currency of the old company code.**

2. You have only posted planning data in the fiscal year.
3. The cost center is not assigned to a fixed asset, work center or HR master record.

Which of the above sentences are false (Please choose the correct option)?

a) 1 and 2 are correct.
b) 2 and 3 are correct.
c) 1 and 3 are correct.
d) 1, 2 and 3 are correct.
e) None of them.

(Only one answer is correct)

Answer – d

Explanation:

You can change the assignments of the organizational units, company code, business area, or profit center during the course of a fiscal year only if the following conditions hold:

- The currency of the new company code is the same as the currency of the old company code.
- You have only posted planning data in the fiscal year.
- The cost center is not assigned to a fixed asset, work center, or HR master record.

12) Define Cost Center Category (Please choose the correct option).

a) It is allowed for only one cost center master data.
b) It is a CO object where costs are incurred.

c) It is an indicator in the cost center master data, which specifies the category for the cost
center.
d) It is an indicator in the controlling area, which specifies what kinds of cost center can be
entered.
e) It is an indicator in the chart of accounts, which specifies the category for the cost center.

(Only one answer is correct)

Answer – c

Explanation:

The cost center category is an indicator in the cost center master data, which specifies the category for the cost center. Examples include administration, production, or sales & distribution. You can use your own cost center categories, or use those supplied by SAP.
Cost center categories enable you to assign the same characteristics to similar cost centers. For example, you can allow particular activity types only for particular cost centers. This is useful to prevent production activities from being posted to administrative cost centers by mistake. You can also use the cost center category for cost calculation, where it controls what percentage of the overheads apply to that cost center category. Cost center category is not a CO object not a part of the COA

13) Define Primary Cost Element (Please choose the correct option).

a) It is the object in CO module that corresponds to the expense and revenue accounts in FI module.
b) It is the object in CO module that are used to record internal value flows like activity allocation, assessments and settlements.
c) It is the object in CO module that is used exclusively to identify internal cost flows and records revenues.
d) It is a revenue element, used in CO and it corresponds to a Balance Sheet Account in FI module.

e) It is a tracing factor that helps to classify the specific activities that are provided by one or more cost centers within a company.

(Only one answer is correct)

Answer – a

Explanation:

A Primary Cost Element is created in financial accounting before it's created in the Controlling module.
Primary cost elements are exclusively used to transfer the finance balances to the controlling module. These can be used to record the primary cost flows and revenues too.
Primary cost element can either be a revenue or an expense element and it corresponds to a P & L account in the FI module. Primary cost element cannot be considered as a tracing factor.

14) True or false?

1. The activity type category is used to determine whether and how an activity type is entered and allocated.
   a) [ ] True. b) [ ] False.

2. The fixed value is only posted in the period in which it is entered.
   a) [ ] True. b) [ ] False.

3. You can create your own list variants for collective processing.
   a) [ ] True. b) [ ] False.

4. SAP recommends that you use the same number interval groups for CO actual and plan transactions.
   a) [ ] True. b) [ ] False.

5. Validation has priority under Substitution.
   a) [ ] True. b) [ ] False.

(More than one answer is True)

Answer – 1: a, 3: a, 5: a

Explanation:

The activity type category is used to determine whether and how an activity type is recorded and allocated. For example, you can allow some activities to be allocated directly, but specify for others that they are either not allocated, or allocated indirectly only.
The fixed value (for example, employees) is carried over from the period in which it is entered to all subsequent periods of the same fiscal year. You only need to enter a new posting if this fixed value changes. The fiscal year total is an average of the period totals.
You can create your own list variants for collective processing. The list variant determines the master data fields that can be processed. You can change the list variant during processing.
SAP recommends that you create different number interval groups for actual and plan transactions.
If you have defined a substitution that contradicts a validation condition, the system informs you of this by displaying a message. We can therefore say that validation has priority, or is "stronger" than substitution.

15) What can we say about period lock (Please choose the correct option)?

a) It is used to lock the business transactions for a combination of company code, fiscal year and document number.

b) It is used to lock the business transactions for a combination of company code, fiscal year and version.

c) It is used to lock the business transactions for a combination of controlling area, fiscal year and version.

d) It is used to lock the business transactions for a combination of company code, fiscal year and plant. e) It is used to lock the business transactions for a combination of company code, fiscal year and purchasing organization.

(Only one answer is correct)

Answer – c

Explanation:

Use the period lock to lock plan and actual business transactions for a combination of controlling area, fiscal year, and version.
You can select individual business transactions for locking from a list of all the actual and plan business transactions.
It is also possible to lock individual business transactions for all the periods of the fiscal year, or all business transactions for individual periods.

16) The following statement(s) is/are correct with holding documents.

a) Free assignment of the designation/ID
b) A document number is assigned
c) No update of the transaction figures
d) Not taken in to account for evaluations/reports

(More than one answer is correct)

Answer – a, c, d

Explanation:

With Hold Document, data which has been entered can be saved temporarily in order to continue the entries at a later time. Documents held by the system do not have to be complete. No account balances are updated and hence the data of the document is not available for evaluation. No document number is assigned.

17) Which of the following are call-up points?

a) Document number
b) Document header
c) Document line item
d) Complete document

(More than one answer is correct)

Answer – b, c, d

Explanation:

System provides the following call up points.

- document header
- document row (doc. Line item)
- entire document

Document number is not a call up point.

18) Profitability Management is related to which SAP R/3 specific module (Please choose the correct option)?

a) Financial Accounting.
b) Materials Management.
c) Controlling.
d) Enterprise Controlling.
e) Sales & Distribution.

(Only one answer is correct)

Answer – d

Explanation:

Profitability management is related with the enterprise controlling module. This is done through the activation of the COPA functionality in profitability management module.
Financial accounting is used to generate reports for external authorities.
Management accounting is used to generate reports for internal purposes.
Materials management module is used to track the inventory movements of an organization.
Sales & distribution module is sued to track the sales invoicing process.

19) Transaction type specifies which of the following are updated:

a) Value fields
b) Depreciation areas
c) Asset balance sheet accounts
d) All of the above

(More than one answer is correct)

Answer – a, b, c, d

Explanation:

Each transaction type is assigned to a transaction type group and to a depreciation area in the asset configuration setting. Asset balance sheet accounts are defined transaction types. The business transactions are subdivided on the basis of the transaction type group into:

- Transactions that influence the acquisition and production costs of fixed assets. These include: Acquisitions, retirements, transfer postings, post-capitalization based on the value fields defined in the asset master record.
- Down payments
- Investment support measures
- Manual depreciation
- Write-ups

20) You can assign an asset to the following Controlling objects:

a) Cost center
b) Internal order
c) Activity type
d) Maintenance order
e) All of the above

(More than one answer is correct)

Answer – a, b, c, d, e

Explanation:

Some information in the asset master record can be managed as time-dependent data. This is of particular significance for cost accounting assignments (for example, cost center, internal order, maintenance order, project or an activity type).

21) Which of the following evaluations types available only for customers?

a) The DSO (Days Sales Outstanding) evaluation
b) The overdue items evaluation
c) Terms Agreed/Terms Taken
d) The currency analysis
e) The due date analysis

(More than one answer is correct)

Answer – a, c

Explanation:

DSO and the terms agreed are evaluation types which are only available for customers. Overdue items evaluation and due date analysis is available for both customers and vendor transactions. The currency analysis is available for GL accounts.

22) What characteristic is needed when we need to calculate profits according to the cost-of-sales approach (Please choose the correct option)?

a) Plant
b) Cost Center
c) Functional Area
d) Dummy Profit Center
e) Operating Concern

(Only one answer is correct)

Answer – c

Explanation:

Functional area is the element to which all overhead costs in Controlling are assigned. Functional areas include:

- Cost centers, assigned through the cost center category
- Orders, assigned through the order type
- WBS elements, assigned through the project type profile
- Cost objects
- Profitability segments, assigned to Sales and Distribution
- Profit centers, derived through account assignments

23) What are the five phases of the Implementation Roadmap (Please choose the correct option)?

a) Global Strategy, Business Process Management of mySAP technology, Development
Management, Software Change Management and Support Desk Management.

b) Project Preparation, Business Blueprint, Realization, Final Preparation and Go Live &
Support.

c) Integrated Product Management, Project Monitoring and Control, Configuration
Management, Supplier Agreement Management and Organizational Effort Management.

d) Supply Chain Management, Customer Relationship Management, Strategic Enterprise
Management, Business Warehouse Management and Advanced Planner Optimizing.

e) Transactions, Logical Component, Documentation, IMG Assignments and Test Cases.

(Only one answer is correct)

Answer – b

Explanation:

The ASAP Roadmap provides the methodology for implementing and continuously optimizing your SAP System. It divides the implementation process into five phases and offers detailed Project Plans. The five stages of the methodology are Project Preparation, Business Blueprint, Realization, Final Preparation and Go Live & Support.

24) Which of the following statement is correct?

a) A company code is not an organizational unit
b) A company code must use business areas
c) A company code can only be linked to one controlling area
d) A company code can have more than one operating Chart of Account

(Only one answer is correct)

Answer – c

Explanation:

A controlling area can have multiple company codes but a single company code can be assigned only to a single controlling area. It is not mandatory to use the business area for a company code. A company code can have only one operating chart of accounts.
A company code is a legal organizational unit.

25) In SAP what is the document principle?

a) It determines the data flow between Financial Accounting and other components of the SAP system
b) It is the set of documents FI is based on
c) It provides an unbroken audit trial from the financial statements to the individual documents
d) It is used to count the number of documents used to during a posting in FI

(Only one answer is correct)

Answer – c

Explanation:

The document principle simply means that the R/3 system records at least one document for every business transaction. In other words, each transaction in SAP R/3 can be traced back to a unique document with the help of a document number. Each document created in SAP R3 system is assigned a unique document number. The document number is assigned by SAP R3 automatically using internal number ranges or users themselves can assign document number using external number ranges.

26) In SAP FI which statements are correct for the chart of accounts?

a) It is possible to assign only two chart of accounts to a company code
b) This is a list of all G/L accounts used by one or several company codes
c) For each G/L account, the chart of accounts contain the account number, account name and the information that control how an account functions and how a G/L account is created in a company code
d) It is possible to assign more than one chart of accounts to a company code

(More than one answer is correct)

Answer – a, b, c, d

Explanation:

Company code can be assigned with two COA: eg. Operating COA and the country COA. The same COA can be used by several company codes. For each G/L account, the chart of accounts contain the account number, account name and the information that control how an account functions and how a G/L account is created in a company code.

27) A company in the SAP structure is:

a) Used the same as a company code
b) A consolidation master record
c) Used to report structures in SAP
d) Used to accumulate company code data for more than one company code

(Only one answer is correct)

Answer – b

Explanation:

A Company Code is the smallest organizational unit for which individual financial statements are created. A company is an attribute in a user's profile. Every user

belongs to one company only.
A company can include one or more company code.
The definition of the company organizational unit is optional.

28) Which of the following are structures of Chart of Accounts?

a) Operating chart of accounts
b) Standard chart of accounts
c) Optional chart of accounts
d) Country specific chart of accounts
e) Group chart of accounts

(More than one answer is correct)

Answer – a, d, e

Explanation:

Charts of accounts can have three different functions in the system:

- **Operating chart of accounts**
  The operating chart of accounts contains the G/L accounts that you use for posting in your company code during daily activities. Financial Accounting and Controlling both use this chart of accounts.
  You have to assign an operating chart of accounts to a company code.

- **Group chart of accounts**
  The group chart of accounts contains the G/L accounts that are used by the entire corporate group. This allows the company to provide reports for the entire corporate group.
  The assigning of a corporate group chart of accounts to a company code is optional.

- **Country-specific chart of accounts**
  The country-specific chart of accounts contains the G/L accounts needed to meet the country's legal requirements. This allows you to provide statements for the country's legal requirements.
  The assigning of a country-specific chart of accounts to a company code is optional.

29) Which of the following statements is incorrect with respect to reconciliation accounts?

(Only one answer is correct)

a) Transactions in the sub-ledgers are posted on the reconciliation accounts in the General Ledger
b) The reconciliation account field can be found in the general data segment of the customer/vendor master record
c) The reconciliation account to be posted to is entered in each customer/vendor master record
d) Balances of the reconciliation accounts can be directly displayed from the main ledger

(Only one answer is correct)

Answer – b

Explanation:

The reconciliation account field can be found in the company code data segment if the customer/vendor master record.

30) Creation of duplicate accounts in A/P can be prevented by using:

a) the match code before creating the new account
b) sensitive dual control
c) switching on automatic duplication check
d) none of the above

(Only one answer is correct)

Answer – a

Explanation:

Match codes can be used to avoid duplicate vendor master creations. Name and address details can be used as match codes.

31) Find the incorrect statements

a) One customer/vendor account can have many reconciliation accounts
b) Direct entries cannot be posted to reconciliation accounts
c) All account groups of customers can have one common no. range
d) One account group of vendors can have up to three no. ranges

(More than one answer is incorrect)

Answer – a, d

Explanation:

Only one reconciliation account can be maintained in the customer/vendor master records. A single number range is attached to a customer/vendor account group.

32) Find the correct statements

a) One customer can have different customer codes in various company codes
b) One customer can have different reconciliation accounts in various company codes
c) Various company codes can have different payment terms with one customer
d) Chart of account segment is mandatory while entering a customer master

(More than one answer is correct)

Answer – a, b, c

Explanation:

A GL account consists of a chart of account segment and a company code segment. Chart of accounts segment is not required at the time of creating a customer master record.

33) What are the segments of the customer master record?

a) Chart of account segment
b) General data segment
c) Purchase organization segment
d) Sales organization data segment

(More than one answer is correct)

Answer – b, d

Explanation:

The segments of the customer master records are: general data segment/company code segment. If a customer is extended to the sales & distribution module, the sales organization segment of the customer master record needs to be activated.

34) The account group of the vendor/customer master records controls the following.

a) The number range of the customer/vendor masters
b) The status of the fields in the only company code segment
c) Characteristics of the one-time customer/vendor master
d) All of the above

(More than one answer is correct)

Answer - a, c

Explanation:

The account group controls the status of the fields in both general data segment and the company code segment.

35) Find the correct statements with respect to the customer master records.

a) If a customer is also a vendor, or vice versa, the payment and the dunning program cannot clear open items against each other.
b) Line item display and open item management are always activated for every customer account.
c) Customer and vendor master records can be created with reference to an existing master record.
d) All of the above

(More than one answer is correct)

Answer - b, c

Explanation:

If a customer is also a vendor, the payment and the dunning program can clear open items against each other. To clear open items, the following steps are required: The vendor account number must be entered in the customer account; the customer account number must be entered in the vendor account. Each company code can decide separately whether it wants to clear open items. If clearing is to be used, you have to select the Clearing with Vendor field in the customer account, or the corresponding field in the vendor account.

36) Select the correct statements with respect to Bank masters.

a) Bank master records are stored centrally in the bank directory and the bank directory can be created in SAP.
b) Bank master records include address data and control data such as the SWIFT Code, postal giro data and bank group
c) There are three ways to create bank master data.
d) All of the above

(More than one answer is correct**)**

Answer - a, b

Explanation:

There are four ways to create bank master records:

- When entering bank information in the customer or vendor master record, or in the Customizing for house banks.
- Using the Create Bank transaction in the Accounts Receivable/Payable master data menu.
- the bank directory can be imported from disk or tape using program
- RFBVALL_0, Country-Specific Transfer of Bank Data. The disk with the bank directory can be obtained from one of the country's banking organizations. The bank directory should be updated regularly.
- Customers that use the lockbox function can create a batch input session that automatically updates customer banking information in the master record.

37) The following are fields in SAP documents:

1. **Document number**
2. **Company code**
3. **Fiscal year**

Documents can be uniquely identified by a combination of:

a) 1 and 2
b) 1 and 3
c) 1, 2 and 3

d) 2 and 3

(Only one answer is correct)

Answer – c

Explanation:

SAP document can be uniquely identified by the document number/company code/fiscal year combination.

38) Select the correct statements with regards to SAP documents.

a) A document is saved for every posting and the document remains as a complete unit in the system until it is archived.
b) A document consists of a header and line items.
c) Maximum line items that can be posted in a document is 999.
d) Document type is maintained in the document header and a document type cannot be overwritten during the document entry.

(More than one answer is correct)

Answer – a, b, c

Explanation:

You can define a document type for each transaction, which then appears as a general default value. You can overwrite this proposed document type at any time as long as the document type field is ready for input during document entry. If you do not define a document type, the system proposes standard document types such as vendor invoice KR for entering vendor invoices and DR for entering customer invoices.

39) The correct statements with respect to Plant and Valuation area are:

a) A plant can be assigned to multiple company codes.
b) A plant can be a central delivery warehouse, a regional sales office, a manufacturing facility, a corporate headquarters, or a maintenance plant.
c) The valuation level defines the valuation area.

d) If the valuation area is the company code all plant stocks of a material are managed in a joint stock account.

(More than one answer is correct)

Answer – b, c, d

Explanation:

The central organizational object in logistics is the plant. A plant is an operating area or branch within a company. A plant must be assigned to a single company code. However, one or more plants can be assigned to the same company code.
If the valuation area is the company code all plant stocks of a material are managed in a joint stock account. The unit price is identical for all plants.
If the valuation area is the plant, the material stocks for each plant can be managed in different accounts. The price can be different for each plant.

40) Identify the correct statements with respect to the material master.

a) Accounting view 1 and 2 can be only maintained in the company code segment.
b) If parts of a material stock are to be valuated differently than other parts, you can use separate valuation.
c) Each part of a material stock is assigned to a valuation type, and the views Accounting 1 and 2.
d) All of the above

(More than one answer is correct)

Answer – b, c

Explanation:

The views Accounting 1 + 2 are maintained at valuation level, that is, either at plant or company code level. These views contain the data for the link to SAP Financials.

41) Identify the correct statements with respect to plant and purchasing organizations.

a) Purchasing organization can be assigned to several plants.
b) Procurement for a plant is carried out by purchasing organizations which are assigned to the plant.
c) The purchasing transactions have to be posted in the company code that is assigned to this plant.
d) All of the above

(More than one answer is correct)

Answer – b, c

Explanation:

A purchasing organization is assigned to only one plant. The purchasing transactions have to be posted in the company code that is assigned to this plant.

One or more purchasing organizations can be assigned to one plant.

42) Out of the parameters given below which can be controlled through the posting key?

a) The design of the entry screens
b) The account type
c) Document reference
d) All of the above

(More than one answer is correct)

Answer – a, b

Explanation:

You also assign the FI posting keys for the debit and credit postings for each posting transaction under Posting Keys. The posting key is a two-place numeric key that controls the entry of document items, such as:

- The account type (vendor, customer, asset, material, or G/L account)
- Credit or debit posting
- The design of the entry screens
-

43) Business area can be assigned by:

a) plant and item division
b) sales area
c) sales organization, distribution channel, and item division
d) All of the above

(More than one answer is correct)

Answer – d

Explanation:

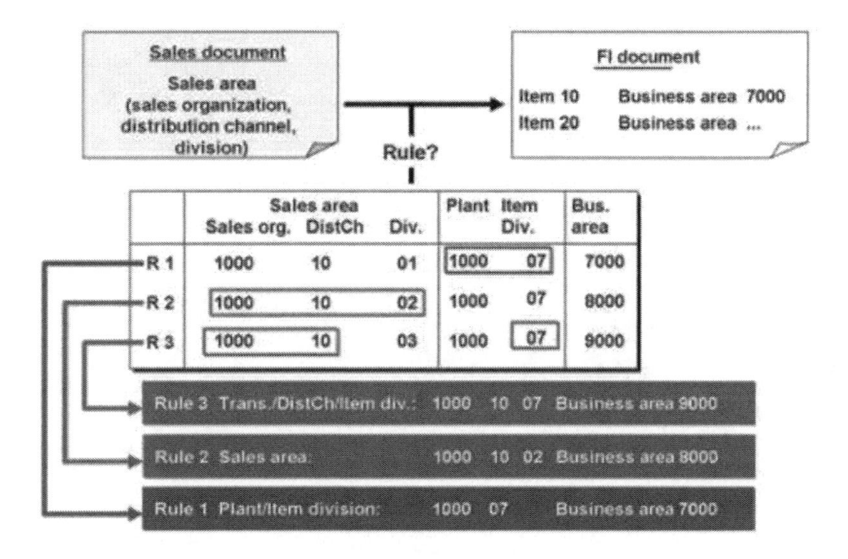

44) The Document Header contains:

a) Only the posting date, document date and document type
b) Only the document date, posting date, currency and company code
c) The document date, posting date, document type, company code, document currency, translation date, etc
d) You can have of the choice of many fields of your own definition

(Only one answer is correct)

Answer – c

Explanation:

Document header contains Document date, posting date, document type, company code, document currency, translation date. Once a document is posted the document type, document currency and the translation date cannot be modified.

45) Which of the following statements about creating customer master records are correct?

a) An account group always gets assigned to a customer.
b) The company code is always a required entry.
c) The account number may be assigned by the user externally.
d) Information on each screen may be defined in configuration as mandatory, suppressed or optional, depending upon the account group.

(More than one answer is correct)

Answer – a, c, d

Explanation:

Company code is not always required when creating customer master records.

Automatic Payments

1) In the payment process, automatic options to the users are:

a) Select open invoice to the paid or collected, and post payment documents
b) Post payment documents and print payment media
c) Select open invoices to be paid or collected, post payment documents and print payment media (please comment on this – Justin has kept pointing out that we have not addressed the printing)

(Only one answer is correct)

Answer – c

Explanation:

Automatic payment process does the following:

- Vendor Invoices are entered directly to the system or can be generated after an invoice verification
- Open invoices are analyzed for due date
- Invoices due for payment are prepared for review
- Payments are approved or modified
- Invoices are paid

Explanation specified in 'c' best describes the automatic options regarding the automatic payment process. Automatic payment cycle clears the invoices and with the payment documents. Once the payment document is created a cheque can be printed for cheque payments. For other types of payments like a bank draft/telegraphic transfer, payment information can be printed.

2) Which of the following are true

a) Any payment block can be removed in payment proposal edit
b) Only line item payment block can be removed during the payment proposal

c) Items that cannot be paid are deleted in the exception list

(Only one answer is correct)

Answer – c

Explanation:

Not all payment blocks can be removed in the payment proposal. For example if a problem arises during the invoice verification process, the invoice is usually blocked for payment. This can be configured in such a way that the block can only be removed during the invoice verification process and not during payment proposal edit.
You can create a payment block in the vendor master record. It prevents any invoices from the vendor from being paid. You can also configure the block so that it has to be removed manually in the master data record before a payment can be processed.
When an AP invoice is entered, an invoice may be blocked for payment. The type of payment block determines whether it can be removed during the payment proposal.
Additional payment blocks can also be defined in the system. Users can specify whether the payment block can be removed when payments are processed

3) Which of the statements on payment program are correct

a) There are four steps in payment process: parameters, proposal program run, print
b) Once the parameters have been specified, the print program is scheduled to generate the print

(Only one answer is correct)

Answer – a

Explanation:

Automatic payment process consists of the following four steps:
Setting parameters, generating a proposal, scheduling the payment run, printing the payment media.

Once parameters are set, however, it is necessary to generate a proposal and schedule the payment run before a separate program is scheduled to print payments.

4) Which of the following statements are true in respect of payment program configuration in all company codes areas.

a) Sending company code and paying company codes are same always.
b) By specifying the vendor/customer, special G/L transaction to be paid, we can process specified special G/L transactions only
c) By activating payment method supplements, we can print and sort payments

(More than one answer correct)

Answer – b, c

Explanation:

If company code A is making payments on behalf of another company code B, then B is the sending company code. If a company code is not specified, the system automatically regards the sending company code as the paying company code. The paying company code is the company code that is responsible for processing the outgoing payments. This company code records the bank postings (A). The sending company code records the sub ledger postings (B). Both companies balance by automatically generating cross company postings.

Vendor/Customer Sp. G/L Transactions to be paid specifies which special general ledger transactions can be processed with the payment program. If activated, Payment Method Supplements allow you to print and sort payments. A payment method supplement comprising two characters that can be assigned to customer/vendor master records. When you enter a document in the system, the relevant data is automatically assigned to the individual items. They also can be manually entered or overwritten in the line item when you enter a document. Payments are sorted and can be printed by supplement.

5) Which of the statements are true in respect to configuration of payment program,
bank determination area

a) Without ranking order, system will not process the payments
b) Bank payment methods combination is must to define ranking order
c) Without maintaining the value date in bank selection, system will not process the payments

(More than one answer correct)

Answer – a, b

Explanation:

The payment program will take the ranking order into consideration when determining which bank to pay from. It will not process payments unless the ranking order is specified. Bank account to process the payment is selected based on the ranking order.

The ranking order cannot be defined unless it is combined with the bank payment method.
Value date can be defaulted through the document date or from the posting date based on the payment term of the business transaction.

6) Say true or false

a) All company codes in the payment run parameters must be in the same country
b) A payment method can only be used if it is entered in the account master record
c) The payment proposal can only be edited, deleted and recreated as often as desired
d) The exception list is a part of the payment proposal

(More than one answer is correct)

Answer - a, c, d

Explanation:

The company codes in a payment run must be in the same country.
For each country, the user must specify payment methods that can be used within that particular country.
Payment method can be defined at the master data level and also at the line item level.
Invoices that match the specified payment parameters but cannot be paid are listed in the exception list which is a part of the payment proposal.

7) Which of the following are the steps involved in the 'payment process'?

a) Setting parameters
b) Generating a proposal
c) Scheduling the payment run
d) Printing the payment media

(More than one answer is correct)

Answer – a, b, c, d

Explanation:

The payment process consists of four steps:

- Setting parameters: In this step, the following questions are asked and answered:
  What is to be paid?
  Which payment methods will be used?
  When will the payment be made?
  Which company codes will be considered?
  How are they going to be paid?

- Generating a proposal: The system starts the proposal run after you have entered the parameters. It generates a list of business partners and open invoices that are due for payment. Invoices can be blocked or unblocked for payment.

- Scheduling the payment run: Once the payment list has been verified, the payment run is scheduled. A payment document is created and the general ledger and sub-ledger accounts are updated.

- Printing the payment media: The accounting functions are completed and a separate print program is scheduled to generate the payment media.

8) Identify the functions of the automatic payment program.

a) Program selects all open invoices to be paid or collected
b) Posts payment documents
c) Only cheque payments are supported through the automatic payment program.
d) All of the above

(More than one answer is correct)

Answer – a, b

Explanation:

Not only cheques but other payment methods like bank transfers, giors can also be supported through the automatic payment program.

9) Which of the following statements are correct with respect to payment programs?

a) There are four steps in payment process: setting parameters, generating a proposal, scheduling the payment run, printing the payment media
b) Each payment run is uniquely identified by the run date, identification and the proposal number
c) The bank details relating to the payment run can be stored in the payment variant.
d) All of the above

(More than one answer correct)

Answer – a, c

Explanation:

Each payment run is uniquely identified by the run date and the payment identification.

10) Which of the following statements with respect to payment program are correct?

a) There are four steps in payment process: setting parameters, generating a proposal, scheduling the payment run, printing the payment media
b) Each payment run is uniquely identified by the run date, identification and the proposal number
c) The bank details relating to the payment run can be stored in the payment variant.
d) All of the above

(More than one answer is correct)

Answer – a, c

Explanation:

Each payment run is uniquely identified by the run date and the payment identification.

11) Find the incorrect statement with respect to the automatic payment program.

a) All company codes in the payment run parameters must be in the same country
b) A payment method can only be used if it is entered in the account master record
c) The payment proposal can only be edited, deleted and recreated as often as desired
d) The exception list is a part of the payment proposal

(Only once answer is incorrect)

Answer – b

Explanation:

Payment method can be maintained in the master record. Also at the time of raising the vendor invoice, the payment method can be entered as a line item.

12) Which of the following statements are correct with respect to the configuration of automatic payments?

a) The paying company code is the company code that is responsible for processing the outgoing payments. This company code records the bank postings. The sending company code records the sub-ledger postings. Both companies balance by automatically generating cross company postings.
b) Vendor/Customer Sp. G/L Transactions to be paid, specifies which special general ledger transactions to be excluded from the payment program.
c) Payment Method Supplements allow you to print and sort payments
d) All of the above

(More than one answer is correct)

Answer – a, c

Explanation:

Vendor/Customer Sp. G/L Transactions to be paid specify which special general ledger transactions can be processed with the payment program. Down payment requests and advances paid to vendors are some examples of the special G/L transactions to be included.

If activated, Payment Method Supplements allow you to print and sort payments. Create a payment method supplement comprising two characters that can be assigned to customer/vendor master records. When you enter a document in the system, the relevant data is automatically assigned to the individual items.

They also can be manually entered or overwritten in the line item when you enter a document. Payments are sorted and can be printed by supplement.

13) Identify the parameters which can be defined for 'payment method for company code.

a) Bank optimization
b) Payment grouping options
c) Maximum and minimum payment amounts
d) Whether foreign currency payments are allowed

(More than one answer is correct)

Answer – a, b, c, d

Explanation:

The following parameters need to be defined for 'payment method for company code'.

- Minimum and maximum payment amounts
- Whether payments abroad and foreign currencies are allowed
- Grouping options
- Bank optimization
- Forms for payment media

14) Identify the components which are taken into consideration when selecting the house bank.

a) Ranking order
b) Value date
c) Accounts for expenses and charges
d) Amounts

(More than one answer is correct)

Answer – a, b, c, d

Explanation:

Following components are taken into consideration when selecting the house bank.

- Ranking order
- Amounts
- Accounts
- Expenses/Charges
- Value date

15) Which of the following parameters need to be configured for the house bank and payment method configuration?

a) Available funds in the bank account
b) Amount available in the incoming payment account
c) Clearing accounts for bills of exchange
d) All of the above

(More than one answer is correct)

Answer – a, c

Explanation:

Amounts available in the outgoing payment accounts are updated. Amount field is not updated automatically after each payment run.

16) Identify the incorrect statements with respect to generating the automatic payment program.

a) All company codes within a payment program must be in the same country
b) If you use more than one payment method in the payment run, the order in which you enter them is not important
c) The posting date is the date when the general ledger is updated with the postings.
d) This date is defaulted from the run date on the previous screen.
e) Once the proposal run is completed, the system generates a single report : the payment proposal list

(More than one answers is incorrect)

Answer – b, d

Explanation:

If you use more than one payment method in the payment run, remember that the order in which you enter them is important. The method entered first has first priority, the next has second priority, and so on. The system makes payments on the basis of highest priority.

Once the proposal run is complete, the system generates two reports: the payment proposal list and the exception list. You can edit these reports online or print them.

The proposal list shows the business partners and the amounts to be paid or received. Depending on the line layout users choose for the screen, the associated document numbers and cash discounts can be displayed. Exceptions are also listed here. Users can drill down several times to view and change the details of the individual payment items.

17) Out of the following which can be found in the exception list?

a) Debit balance exists for the vendor
b) Invoice is blocked for payment
c) Invalid payment method specified
d) All of the above

(More than one answer is correct)

Answer – d

Explanation:

Exception List

- **Items that cannot be paid are detailed on the exception list**
- Possible reasons:
  - Invoice is blocked
  - Invalid data in the master record
  - Invalid payment method
  - Invalid house bank
  - Payment amount is less than the minimum amount specified for payment
  - Not enough money in the house bank per configuration
  - Debit balance

18) Identify the correct statements with respect to the automatic payment program.

a) After the payment run is created, it can be edited by an accounting clerk.
b) The document type for payment documents is defined in the company specific specifications for the payment method.
c) The value date of the clearing document is calculated by adding the days to value date to the posting date.
d) If payments are made for individual business areas, the bank posting is made for the business area to which the paid items belong.

(More than one answer is correct)

Answer – a

Explanation:

After the payment run is created, it can be edited by accounting clerks. Users can assign an accounting clerk to a customer/vendor by entering the clerk's key in the customer / vendor master data. When editing the payment proposal, you can enter the key of a specific clerk to show only the customer / vendor payments that are assigned to the clerk.

The document type for payment documents is defined in the country-specific specifications for the payment method. For cross-company-code payments, you can enter a further document type that is used for the clearing postings. Both document types must be defined using internal number assignment.

If payments are made for individual business areas, the bank posting is made for the business area to which the paid items belong. If payments are not made for specific business area, you can specify the business area for the bank postings. In all other cases, the postings to the bank subaccounts are carried out without reference to business areas.

19) The print program :

a) assigns check numbers to payment documents
b) updates only the payment documents with the check information
c) prints checks and accompanying documents
d) does all of the above

(More than one answer is correct)

Answer – a, c

Explanation:

The print program updates the payment documents and original invoice documents with the check information. If you are using check management, you have to use check lots to print checks. Checks are managed in batches, or lots. If you are using pre numbered checks from the bank, specify the check number ranges in lots. Otherwise, start the check numbering from 1.

20) Find the correct statements with respect to the debit balance check.

a) The check offsets all the due debit items without an incoming payment method against the proposed payments.
b) If the resulting debit balance or credit balance is less than the minimum payment amount, the payments are added to the exception list and the account is placed on a list of blocked accounts
c) The debit balance check can be carried out after a payment proposal has been created
d) All of the above

(More than one answer is correct)

Answer – d

Explanation:

The debit balance check can be carried out after a payment proposal has beencreated. The check offsets all the due debit items without an incoming payment method against the proposed payments. If the resulting debit balance or credit balance is less than the minimum payment amount, the payments are added to the exception list and the account is placed on a list of blocked accounts. The relevant accounts remain blocked even if the payment proposal is then deleted. This means that the payments for the blocked accounts are not made in the subsequent update run with the same payment run identification. The blocks are not removed until the proposal is created again with the same identification.

Blocked accounts can be released manually.

21) The documents involved in a payment process are:

1. Vendor invoice
2. Payment documents
3. Checks

a) 1 & 2correct
b) 2 & 3correct
c) 1 & 3correct
d) 1, 2, & 3 are all correct

(More than one answer is correct)

Answer – d

Explanation:

There are three documents involved in the payment process.

- Vendor invoice
- Payment documents
- Checks (preprinted checks / check number generated from the system)

Automatic Dunning

1) Which of the statements are true when running the dunning program

a) We can edit proposal
b) We cannot delete the proposal
c) We can recreate the proposal until the dunning clerk is satisfied with the result
d) After completing the dunning proposal list, dunning data is updated in the master records of respective customer/ vendor

(More than one answer correct)

Answer – a, c

Explanation:

During the dunning run, the system chooses the accounts and checks them for items that are overdue. Finally, a check is made whether reminders have to be sent and dunning levels are allocated. All dunning data is saved in one dunning proposal.

The dunning proposal can be edited, deleted, and re-created as often as required until the accounting clerk is satisfied with the result.
Dunning notices can be printed and dunning data is updated in the master records and associated documents.

2) Which of the following statements are true

a) One time accounts cannot be dunned
b) We can assign two dunning procedures to customer master records
c) Dunning procedure can process only standard transactions
d) Interest can be posted at the time of dunning run

Answer – all answers incorrect

Explanation:

One-time-accounts also have a dunning procedure that is valid for all one-time customers.
You can define any number of dunning procedures. The SAP system contains several predefined dunning procedures, which you can use as templates for other procedures.
The dunning procedure can process standard and/or special G/L transactions.
By using the interest indicator, interested can be calculated and posted to the customer account.

3) The maximum dunning levels can be defined in dunning procedure are:

a) Four
b) Six
c) Nine

(Only one answer correct)

Answer – c

Explanation:

Each dunning procedure contains up to nine dunning levels. The dunning notice wording is usually influenced by the dunning level. The higher the dunning level, the stronger the formulation in the dunning text. Each item to be dunned is assigned a dunning level according to its days in arrears. For invoice-related credit memos, the dunning level of the invoice is used. From one dunning run to another the dunning level can only be raised by one, that is, no dunning levels can be skipped.

4) An item whose days in arrears are smaller or identical to the grace periods, dunning program will consider for the dunning notice.
TRUE/FALSE

Answer – false

Explanation:

The minimum number of days in arrears is set as a default in the system: The system proposes the Line Item Grace Period as the first dunning level. For all further dunning levels, the system adds the dunning interval in days to the days in arrears of the previous dunning level.

5) What information does a dunning run change?

a) The date of the 'last dunning run' in the customer master record
b) The dunning level in the customer master record
c) The dunning level in documents for which dunning notices are created
d) Form (lay out set) specifications in the customer master record for the text in the next dunning letter
e) The dunning procedure in the customer master record for the next dunning run

(More than one answer is correct)

Answer – a, b, c

Explanation:

Last dunning date/dunning level is stored in the customer master record.
Neither the form spec nor the dunning procedure for the next dunning run are changed during a dunning run.

From one dunning run to another the dunning level is raised by one and no dunning levels can be skipped.

6) Which of the following statements are false

a) We cannot specify per dunning level that interest is to be calculated

b) We cannot print a dunning notice in a legal dunning procedure, although no further account movements have occurred
c) We can set a minimum amount for dunning charges on each dunning level

(More than one answer correct)

Answer – a, b

Explanation:

For dunning interest to be calculated, you have to enter an interest indicator. You can print a dunning notice in a legal dunning procedure, even though no further account movements have occurred.

Minimum amounts for dunning charges cannot be set on each dunning level.

7) What are the fields by which every dunning program run is identified?

a) Run date
b) Program number
c) Customer number
d) Identification

(More than one answer is correct)

Answer – a, d

Explanation:

If you have not received payments from your customers by the net due date, you have to check whether dunning notices should be sent. You can formulate the first dunning notice as a friendly reminder. If your customer still fails to pay, you might want to formulate the text more strongly. The Accounting manager wants to find out how the dunning program can help him do this. First, he would like a general overview of the dunning procedure. Dunning run can be uniquely identified by the run date and the identification name.

8) Items that are to be dunned are grouped together in dunning notices if they have the same of following:

a) Company code
b) Dunning area
c) Account
d) Number range

(More than one answer is correct)

Answer – a, b, c

Explanation:

Items that are to be dunned are grouped together in dunning notices as long as they have the same:

- Company code
- Dunning area (if dunning areas are used)
- Account

Items in a one-time account are grouped together in one dunning notice if they have the same address.

9) Find the correct sequence for generating the dunning procedure.

a) Maintain parameters → Change dunning notices → Schedule dunning run →Start dunning printout
b) Maintain parameters → Schedule dunning run → Start dunning printout → Change dunning notices
c) Maintain parameters → Schedule dunning run → Change dunning notices → Start dunning printout
d) Schedule dunning run → Maintain parameters → Start dunning printout → Change dunning notices

(Only one answer correct)

Answer – c

Explanation:

First, the correct parameters need to be specified and the next step is to schedule the dunning run. Once the job is completed the user can change the dunning notices and finally the dunning printouts can be generated.

10) Identify the correct statements with respect to automatic dunning procedure.

a) The dunning procedure controls how dunning is carried out.
b) You can define up to a maximum of four dunning procedures.
c) The dunning procedure can process standard and/or special G/L transactions.
d) All of the above

(More than one answer is correct)

Answer – a, c

Explanation:

You can define any number of dunning procedures. The SAP system contains several predefined dunning procedures, which you can use as templates for other procedures. One-time-accounts also have a dunning procedure that is valid for all one-time customers.

11) Dunning program settings are divided in to how many categories?

a) 3

b) 4
c) 5
d) 6

(Only one answer is correct)

Answer – d

Explanation:

The dunning program settings are divided in to six categories:

- Dunning procedures
- Dunning levels
- Expenses/Charges
- Minimum amounts
- Dunning texts
- Environment

12) Identify the attributes which need to be defined in the dunning process

a) Intervals at which the accounts that use this procedure are to be dunned.
b) Grace periods for each customer
c) Interest indicator
d) All of the above

(More than one answer is correct)

Answer – a, c

Explanation:

The grace period should be specified for each line item. An item whose number of days in arrears is less than or equal to the number of grace days is not considered due for this dunning notice.

13) Find the incorrect statement with respect to dunning levels?

a) The system proposes the Line Item Grace Period as the second dunning level.
b) For each dunning level, you can specify that interest is to be calculated.
c) You can print a dunning notice in a legal dunning procedure, even though no further account movements have occurred.
d) For each dunning level, you can specify that interest is to be calculated.

(Only one answer incorrect)

Answer – a

Explanation:

The minimum number of days in arrears is set as a default in the system: The system proposes the Line Item Grace Period as the first dunning level. For all further dunning levels, the system adds the dunning interval in days to the days in arrears of the previous dunning level.

You can specify that interest is to be calculated for each dunning level.

If you choose the Always Dun option, dunning notices are printed even if the dunning proposals have not changed since the last dunning run. A dunning proposal is considered changed if it fulfills at least one of the following criteria:

- At least one item has reached a different dunning level
- A new item was added to the dunning notice
- The dunning level of the account was changed

14) Select the correct statement with respect to dunning charges.

a) Dunning charges can be either a fixed amount or a percentage of the dunned amount.
b) You cannot set a minimum amount for dunning charges
c) Dunning charges are defined for each currency and depend on the dunning level.
d) All of the above

(More than one answer is correct)

Answer – a, c

Explanation:

Dunning charges are defined for each currency and depend on the dunning level. You can use the word processing features to print these charges on dunning forms. The dunning charge can be either a fixed amount or a percentage of the dunned amount. If you have defined a percentage dunning charge, you cannot enter a fixed dunning charge at the same time. You can set a minimum amount at each dunning level.

15) Which are the parameters that can be specified in the dunning run?

a) Company code or a range of company codes
b) Documents posted to date
c) Range of customer and vendor accounts
d) Free selections

(More than one answer is correct)

Answer – a, b, c, d

Explanation:

Which company codes?

- **Company code, such as selection range for individual values**

Which accounts?

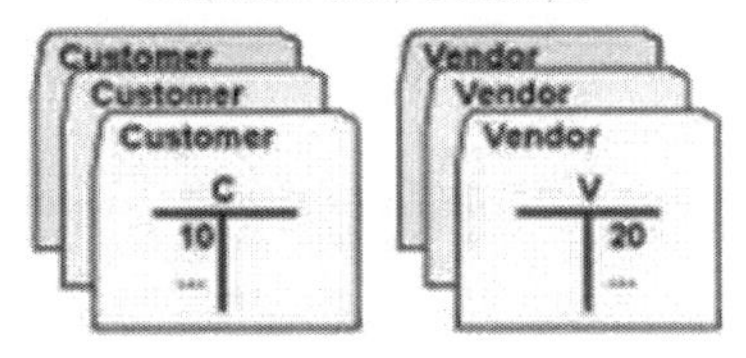

- **Range of customer / vendor accounts**
- **Free selection**

Which documents?

- ***Document posted to* date**
- **Free selection**

16) The correct sequence to generate the dunning run is:

a) Dunning line items → Accounts selection →Account dunning
b) Account selection → Dunning line items → Account dunning
c) Account dunning → Account selection → Dunning line items
d) Account dunning → Dunning line items → Account selection

(Only one answer correct)

Answer – b

Explanation:

The dunning run can be divided into the three steps.
Step 1: Account Selection. In this step the program checks which accounts shall be considered in the dunning run according to the parameters and configuration.

Step 2: Dun Line Items. In this step, the system checks which line items are overdue in the selected accounts and which dunning level should be applied.

Step 3: Dun Accounts. In this step, the system checks whether payments have to be dunned for an account and, if so, which dunning level should be used.

17) Which of the following statements are correct with respect to the account selection in the dunning run?

a) A dunning procedure must be entered in the master data
b) The date of the last dunning run entered in the account must be earlier thanthe dunning interval date of the dunning procedure.
c) If you want the payment terms in a credit memo to apply, you have to enter V in the Invoice reference field
d) Usually the payment terms of a credit memo do not apply

(More than one answer is correct)

Answer – a, b, c, d

Explanation:

Usually the payment terms of a credit memo do not apply. Instead, the following rules are valid:

- If a credit memo is invoice-related, it has the same due date as the invoice.
- All other credit memos are due at the base line date.

If you want the payment terms in a credit memo to apply, you have to enter V in the Invoice reference field.

18) Identify the incorrect statement with respect to the dunning dates.

a) Due date is the day by which the liabilities should have been paid.
b) Dunning date is the day when the overdue items are dunned.
c) If line item grace periods have been defined in the line items, only those items that are still overdue after the grace days have been deducted are dunned
d) Every dunned item must be overdue, but not all overdue items are dunned.

(Only one answer incorrect)

Answer – c

Explanation:

Usually all items which are overdue at the date of issue have to be dunned. If line item grace periods have been defined in the dunning procedure, only those items that are still overdue after the grace days have been deducted are dunned.

19) The following statements refer to dunning levels and dunning statements. Which of them are correct?

a) Each dunning procedure contains up to five dunning levels.
b) Each item to be dunned is assigned a dunning level according to its days in arrears. For invoice-related credit memos, the dunning level of the invoice is used.
c) The total amount of all the items in an account with a certain dunning level must be greater than a defined minimum amount. The relationship between the total amount and the total open items must be greater than a minimum percentage.
d) The account can only be dunned if at least one item has reached the maximum days in arrears per account.

(More than one answer is correct)

Answer – b, c

Explanation:

Each dunning procedure contains up to nine dunning levels.
The account can only be dunned if at least one item has reached the minimum days in arrears per account.

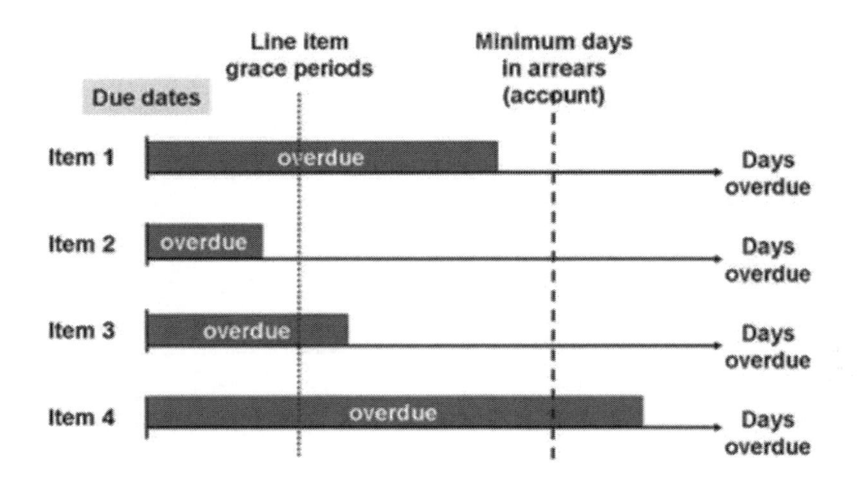

20) Items that are to be dunned are grouped together in dunning notices as long as they have the same :

a) Company code
b) Dunning area
c) Account
d) All of the above

(Only one answer is correct)

Answer – d

Explanation:

Items that are to be dunned are grouped together in dunning notices as long as they have the same address.

21) Identify the correct information that can be captured in the correspondent types.

a) Account number
b) Document number
c) Intercompany relationships
d) All of the above

(More than one answer is correct)

Answer – d

Explanation:

Following information is defined in the correspondence types:

- Required information : Account number & Document number
- Additional text
- Number of data fields required
- Intercompany relationship with the correspondence company code

Correspondence

1) Which of the statements are true

a) We can calculate interest on G/L account under interest on arrears method
b) Each interest id must be assigned an interest calculation type
c) R/3 uses same interest calculation indicator for each combination of interest variables, such as calculation frequency, calendar types, currency

(Only one answer is correct)

Answer – b

Explanation:

Interest calculation types set basic parameters used in calculation. To calculate interest for an account (G/L, customer, vendor), the master data for that account must include the interest calculation indicator that applies.

For customers/vendors interest can be calculated on the arrears method but not for a GL account.

Interest calculation program identifies the items on which interest is to be calculated according to the rules defined in the interest indicator, and any additional specifications you make when executing the program. The rules you enter determine the items and transaction for which interest can be calculated, such as: cleared or open items/ Credit and debit items or only debit items, all clearing transactions or only those with a payment. R/3 uses different interest calculation indicators for each combination of interest variables, such as calculation frequency, calendar types, currency.

Logistics Integration

1) **Consider the following processes that occur in R/3 system:**

1. **It has been generated a goods receipt for a purchase order.**
2. **It has been created an invoice receipt for a purchase order.**
3. **It has been posted an asset.**
4. **It has been created a SD billing document, with a valuated project stock.**
5. **It has been created a SD billing document with a Sales Order.**

**How can the profit center be determined for each case, respectively (Please choose the
correct option)?**

a) indirectly, indirectly, indirectly, indirectly, indirectly
b) dynamically, indirectly, indirectly, dynamically, indirectly
c) dynamically, dynamically, dynamically, dynamically, indirectly
d) indirectly, indirectly, dynamically, dynamically, indirectly
e) indirectly, indirectly, indirectly, dynamically, indirectly

(Only one answer correct)

Answer – d

Explanation:

When a goods receipt is created for a purchase order, the profit center is always determined indirectly, according the profit center defined in the purchase order. When an invoice receipt is created for a purchase order, the profit center is always determined indirectly, according the profit center defined in the purchase order. When an asset is posted, the profit center is always determined dynamically (Overhead Cost Order OR Cost center of the asset). When a SD billing document is created with a valuated project stock, the profit center is determined dynamically from the WBS element contained in the actual SD billing document. When a SD billing document is created with a sales order, the profit center is always determined indirectly, according the profit center defined in the sales order.

2) Smith is the Finance Manager of a repetitive manufacturing organization. Just after signing up with customers the company requires a bank guarantee from all customers. The credit department will determine the amount of the bank guarantee. Smith should record this bank guarantee as a :

a) Noted Item
b) A Free Offsetting Entry
c) Automatic Offsetting Entry
d) Special Advance received from a customer

(Only one answer is correct)

Answer – c

Explanation:

Bank guarantees are usually included in the notes to financial statements and are transactions which are always posted on the same offsetting account. Therefore a bank guarantee needs to be recorded as an Automatic Offsetting entry. This is a memorandum entry.

Noted Items re individual account assignments which are only used to remind the respective department of due payments or payments to be made and are not intended to be displayed in the general ledger.

Free offsetting entries are part of the financial statements. Example: the bank posting of a received down payment.

Special advance received from a customer would always generate a double entry and cannot be considered as a memorandum entry.

3) Find the incorrect statements with respect to the three way match in SAP.

a) The first step is to create a PO in the system. This activity is carried out exclusively in MM module. No postings are made in Financials. Commitments are recorded.

b) At the time of Goods Receipt a material document is created in the Materials Management module to update the stock. The GR/IR account is debited in the financial module.
c) During the Invoice Verification, the vendor invoice is created in Materials Management module and, at the same time, a document is created in Financials.
d) The GR/IR account can be created as a line item managed account

(More than one answer correct)

Answer – a, c

Explanation:

A material document is created in Materials Management to update stock. At the same time, a document is created in Financials. The debit entry is posted to the material stock account or the consumption account and the credit entry is posted to the goods/invoice receipt clearing account. A common abbreviation for the clearing account is GR/IR account. The GR/IR account should be created as an open item managed account to set off the Goods Receipt against the Invoice verification.

4) Which of the following sequences is correct in processing down payments in the MM module?

a) PO creation →Goods Receipt →Down payment Request →Invoice verification →Down payment clearing
b) PO creation → Down payment Request → Invoice verification →Goods Receipt → Down payment clearing
c) Down payment Request → PO creation →Goods Receipt → Invoice verification →Down payment clearing
d) PO creation → Down payment Request → Goods Receipt → Invoice verification →Down payment clearing

(Only one answer correct)

Answer – d

Explanation:

- The purchase order is posted.
- The vendor would like to have a down payment from us for this purchase order. The down payment request is entered together with the order number (Purchasing Document field) in Financials and can then be made, for instance by means of the payment program.
- The goods are received and posted as usual with reference to the purchase order number.
- The vendor sends the invoice. It is posted via Logistics Invoice Verification with reference to the purchase order number. A message appears that there is a down payment for this order.

- The down payment is cleared as usual. The invoice number is also submitted and the respective purchase order number is displayed in the overview of down payments.

5) Find the incorrect statement with regard to the sales transactions.

a) A sales order is a sales document that does not result in any postings in financial accounting.
b) A sales order does not generate any finance documents. A delivery document is created on the day of the delivery. The delivery can only be billed once the goods have been taken from the stock and posted as a goods issue.
c) A goods issue creates documents in both MM & FI modules. The accounting document credits the sales account and debits the stock account.
d) The last phase of the sales transaction is the billing. A billing document is generated in SD and the customer receives a printed invoice

(Only one answer incorrect)

Answer – c

Goods issue creates documents in both MM & FI modules. However, the sales account is debited and the stock account is credited.

6) You are required to explain the SD down payment request process to an accounts executive. How would you explain the process?

a) Down payments cannot be stored in the sales order.
b) A down payment request is sent to the customer for the respective due date.
c) The down payment request (Sales) is automatically posted in Financial Accounting (FI) as down payment request (posted as noted item; special G/L indicator F).

d) The FAZ billing type is used to create the down payment request.
e) Down payment requests are normally made in Sales and Distribution as part of a billing plan. The result is a letter to the customer in which the anticipated amount and the due date are specified

(More than one answer correct)

Answer – b, c, d

Explanation:

Down payments can be stored in the sales order.

7) Which transactions generate entries in both FI & MM modules?

a) Purchase order
b) Goods receipt
c) Purchase Requisition
d) Invoice verification

(More than one answer correct)

Answer – b, d

Explanation:

A purchase order or purchase requisition only generates entries in the MM module. No financial entries are generated.
Goods receipt & invoice verification update both the MM and the FI modules.

8) Identify the correct statements with respect to the main business processes below and their integration in SAP.

a) Goods receipt is the recording of the movement of materials into the warehouse. In SAP, a financial document which updates the inventory account and an accrued liability account is created at the time of goods receipt.
b) The Invoice receipt and verification process compares the vendor invoice with the purchase order and goods receipt. However, the corresponding financial transaction must be entered through the financial module in SAP.
c) In SAP, payment processing reduces the liability to a vendor and a company code cash balance.
d) The sales order is the basis for the sales transaction. A sales order must be created as the first step of a sales transaction after the customer has placed an order.

(More than one answer correct)

Answer – a, c, d

Explanation:

The Invoice receipt and verification process compares the vendor invoice with the purchase order and goods receipt. Financial transactions are automatically generated by the system.

9) Select the correct statements with respect to three step reconciliation.

a) Generating a purchase order transaction takes place exclusively in purchasing management. Nothing is posted in SAP ERP Financials.
b) The goods receipt/invoice receipt (GR/IR) account is managed as a line item managed account.
c) The vendor invoice is posted in purchasing management and an accounting document is created at the same time that is used to post the invoice amount to the goods receipt/invoice receipt account (credit) and the vendor account (debit).
d) All of the above.

(More than one answer is correct)

Answer – a, b

Explanation:

The vendor invoice is posted in purchasing management and an accounting document is created at the same time that is used to post the invoice amount to the goods receipt/invoice receipt account (debit) and the vendor account (credit).

10) Automatic postings in the materials management module can be defined in:

1. **The Material valuation area**
2. **Invoice verification**
3. **Vendor invoice generation**
4. **All of the above**

Which of the following statements is correct?

a) 1& 2 are correct
b) 2 & 3 are correct
c) 1 & 3 are correct
d) All of the above are correct

(Only one answer is correct)

Answer – b

Explanation:

The processes in Materials Management for which automatic postings can be configured are located in the inventory management, invoice verification, and material valuation areas. This also includes goods movements that are initiated by processes in manufacturing (goods issue for a production order, for example) and sales (goods issue for a sales order).

11) Where can you specify the account determination?

a) Chart of accounts
b) Valuation area
c) Valuation type
d) All of the above

(More than one answer is correct)

Answer – d

Explanation:

Chart of accounts - You have to configure account determination separately for each chart of accounts.

Valuation area - You can configure account determination dependent on the valuation area for some transactions, such as consumption postings.

Valuation type - If you use split valuation for certain materials, you can also configure account determination dependent on the valuation type.

12) Identify the correct statements with respect to the valuation and account determination in the MM module.

a) G/L account assignment (account determination) is always dependent on the chart of accounts.
b) When you enter the MM business processes, the valuation area (plant or company code) is known.
c) If you use split valuation for a material, you cannot valuate the partial stocks of that material separately.
d) All of the above

(More than one answer is correct)

Answer – a, b

Explanation:

If you use split valuation for a material, you can valuate the partial stocks of that material separately, as well as manage them in different accounts.

G/L account assignment (account determination) is always dependent on the chart of accounts. You assign the chart of accounts to a company code in FI Customizing.

When you enter the MM business processes, the valuation area (plant or company code) is known. You can choose in Customizing whether the valuation area is equivalent to the company code or the plant. You have to define this setting before you create materials and before you enter transactions in MM inventory management

13) Which of the following statements are correct with respect to the Valuation area?

a) Material stocks can only be valuated at the plant level
b) If you choose the plant as the valuation level, each plant is a valuation area.
c) You can assign the G/L accounts for automatic account assignment dependent on plant
d) All of the above

(Only one answer is correct)

Answer – b

Explanation:

The valuation area is an organizational unit in logistics that subdivides an enterprise for the purpose of uniform and complete valuation of material stocks.
In the SAP system, you define the level at which the material stocks are to be valuated at your company:

- At company code level
- At plant level

The chart of accounts is part of the key in the table for automatic account determination, since the meaning of a G/L account can differ between charts of accounts.

14) Identify the correct statements with respect to the valuation area and account determination.

a) Valuation grouping codes either represent detailed differentiation within a chart of accounts nor correspond to a chart of accounts
b) Within a chart of accounts, valuation areas with the same account assignment are assigned to the same valuation grouping codes.
c) Automatic account determination can be configured only for a single chart of accounts
d) All of the above

(More than one answer is correct)

Answer – a, b

Explanation:

The diagram below shows a company in which several company codes use the same chart of accounts, while one company code uses a different chart of accounts. Automatic account determination has to be configured separately at least for each chart of accounts.

Valuation Level: Company Code

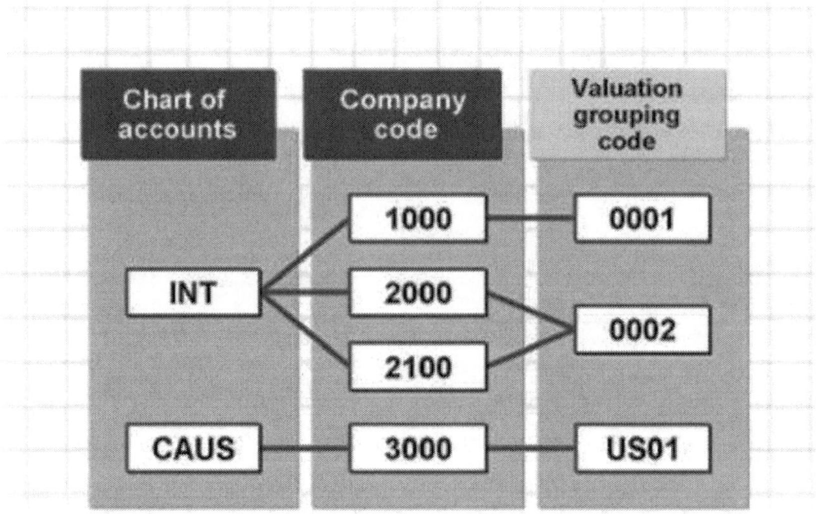

15) Find the correct statements with respect to the materials master.

1. The price control indicator can be configured as a default value or as a fixed value.
2. The type of inventory management for a material type can be defined separately for each valuation area.
3. You can define automatic account determination material-specifically
4. All of the above

(Only one answer is correct)

Answer – d

Explanation:

The price control indicator can be configured as a default value (that is, a suggestion that can be overwritten) or a fixed value. Stock and inventory accounts are assigned using the valuation classes. Account category references establish the links between valuation classes and material types.
You can define automatic account determination material-specifically. This enables you to post the receipt of a raw material to a different stock account than receipt of trading goods, for example - all dependent on the material type. You may also want to define different stock accounts for materials that are dependent solely on the procurement type (produced in-house or procured externally).

16) Identify the correct statements with respect to valuation class.

a) The valuation class is a key for grouping materials with the same account determination.
b) You enter the valuation class in the purchasing data of a material.
c) The valuation classes permitted depend on the material type. Several valuation classes can be permitted for one material type.
d) All of the above

(More than one answer is correct)

Answer – a, c

Explanation:

The valuation class is entered in the accounting data of a material.

Valuation class

- Key for account determination that enables differentiation for G/L account dependent on the material
- You assign materials to a valuation class per valuation area in the accounting view
- You can define (indirect) restrictions by assigning the permitted valuation classes to the material type

Clnt	Chrt/Accts	Transaction	VGC	AG	ValClass	DEBIT G/L acct	CREDIT G/L acct
400	INT	BSX	0001	---	3000	300 000	300 000
400	INT	GBB	0001	VBR	3000	400 000	400 000
400	INT	BSX	0001	---	7900	790 000	790 000
400	INT	GBB	0001	VBR	7900	890 000	890 000

17) Goods receipts must be valuated before they are posted in Financial Accounting.
The type of valuation is defined by the entry in the price control indicator in the material master record. The price control indicator can be:

1. **Moving average price**
2. **Standard price**

Which of the following is correct?

a) 1 only
b) 2 only
c) 1 & 2
d) None of the above

(Only one answer is correct)

Answer – c

Explanation:

Moving average price - The goods received are valuated based on the purchase order price. The moving average price is calculated by dividing the total value by the total inventory. It is used as the clearing price for goods issues.

Standard price - The standard price is entered in the material master record. The goods received are valuated with the standard price. Any differences between the valuated goods received and the purchase order amount is posted to a price difference account.

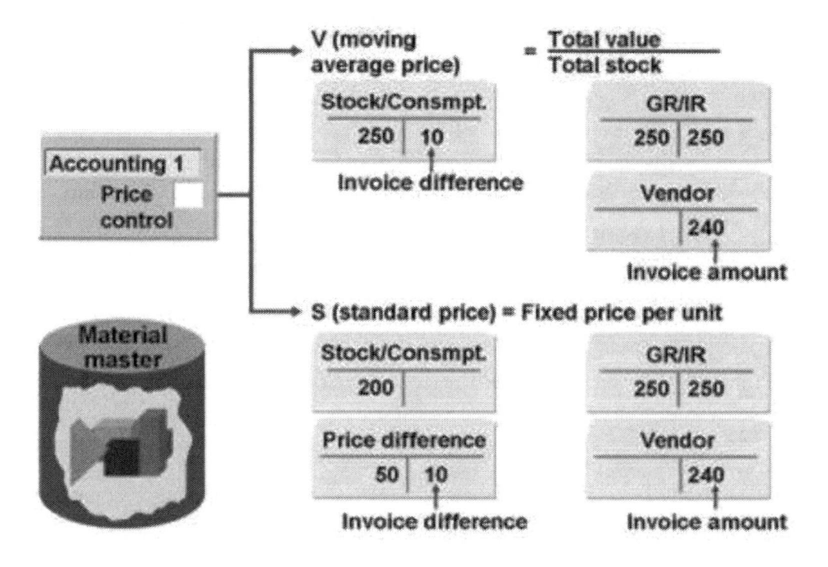
V (moving
average price)
= Total value
Total stock
Stock/Consmpt.
250 10
Invoice difference
GR/IR
250 250
Vendor
240
Invoice amount
Accounting 1
Price
control
S (standard price) = Fixed price per unit
Material
master
Stock/Consmpt.
200
GR/IR
250 250
Price difference
50 10
Invoice difference
Vendor
240
Invoice amount

18) Automatic account assignment depends on the following:

a) Chart of accounts
b) Valuation area
c) Valuation type
d) All of the above

(Only one answer is correct)

Answer – d

Explanation:

Rules let you define whether the assignment of G/L accounts for a transaction with automatic account assignment is dependent on:

- The valuation grouping codes
- The account groupings (not possible for every posting key)
- The valuation class

19) Out of the parameters specified below which parameters are taken in to account in setting up for the automatic account determination?

a) Chart of account of the company code
b) Valuation grouping code of the plant or company code
c) Valuation class of the material
d) Transaction key from the value string, possibly with account grouping

(More than one answer is correct)

Answer – a, b, c, d

Explanation:

The following system parameters (account determination keys) are taken into account in the settings for automatic account determination:

- Chart of account of the company code
- Valuation grouping code of the plant or company code
- Valuation class of the material

- Transaction key from the value string, possibly with account grouping

You can assign the G/L accounts for your business processes dependent on these parameters.

20) Identify the correct statements with respect to a sales organization.

a) A sales organization must be assigned to exactly one company code.
b) Only one sales organization can be assigned to one company code
c) Goods are sold by sales organizations using different distribution channels
d) All of the above

(More than one answer is correct)

Answer – a, c

Explanation:

A sales organization must be assigned to exactly one company code. Several sales organizations can be assigned to the same company code.
Goods are sold by sales organizations using different distribution channels (for example, retail, wholesale, direct merchandizing). A distribution channel can be used by several sales organizations.

21) Identify the correct statements.

a) A sales organization, a distribution channel, and a division can make up a sales area.
b) Divisions can be assigned to sales organizations.
c) Sales transactions are posted automatically in the company code assigned to the sales organization
d) All of the above

(More than one answer is correct)

Answer – d

Explanation:

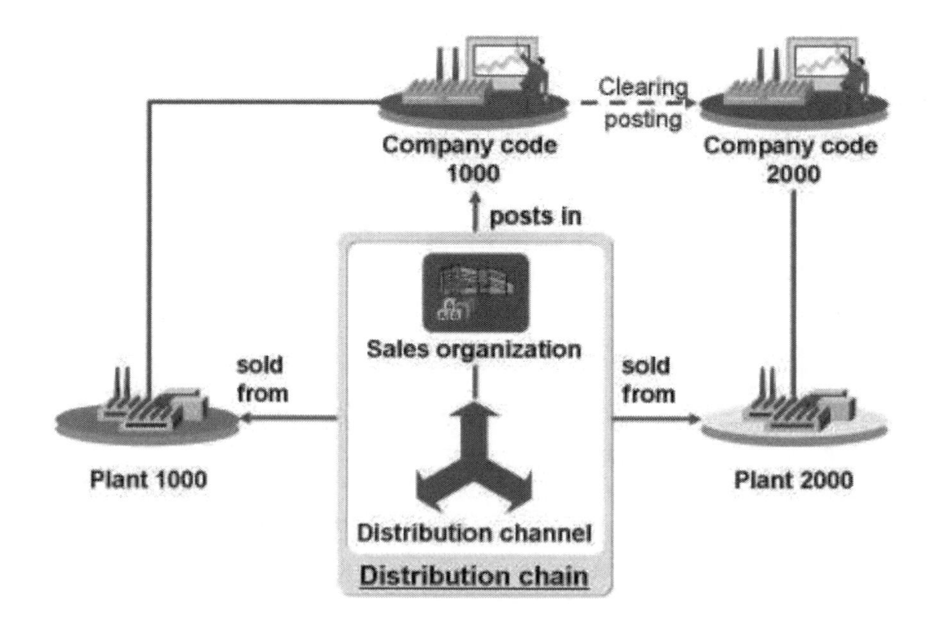

22) Identify the correct statements with respect to the sales process.

a) The sales order is a sales order management document and generates posting in Financial Accounting
b) Once the customer order has been entered, the system carries out an availability check for the required delivery date.
c) On the day of shipping, a delivery document is created.
d) All of the above

(More than one answer is correct)

Answer – b, c

Explanation:

The sales order is a sales order management document and does not lead to posting in Financial Accounting.
On the day of shipping, a delivery document is created. The delivery can only be billed once the goods have been picked from the warehouse inventory and posted as a goods issue.

23) Which of the following billing data can be changed before the accounting document is created?

a) Billing date
b) Pricing
c) Account determination
d) Message determination

(More than one answer is correct)

Answer – a, b, c, d

Explanation:

The system forwards billing data to Financial Accounting in invoices, credit memos, and debit memos and posts this data to the accounts determined.
All of the above billing data can be changed before the accounting document is created.

24) Identify the correct statements.

a) Documents in Financial Accounting can be differentiated by document type.
b) The billing documents that you want to group together in the invoice list must already be billed and forwarded to Financial Accounting.
c) When the invoice list is created, the existing reference number in the individual billing documents cannot be overwritten by the number of the invoice list.
d) All of the above

(More than one answer is correct)

Answer – a, b

Explanation:

When the invoice list is created, the existing reference number in the individual billing documents is overwritten by the number of the invoice list. As a result, you can also specify the invoice list number when you post the payment receipt.

Special G/L Transactions

1) Individual value adjustment for doubtful receivables are possible

a) Through special G/L transaction
b) Through normal transaction
c) Both of the above

(Only one answer correct)

Answer – a

Explanation:

Disputed or doubtful receivables are entered as individual value adjustments when preparing the balance statements for year-end closing. The special general ledger procedure is suitable here, since the transaction is entered in the customer account as well as posted to the special G/L account, Individual Value Adjustments for Receivables.

2) Which of the following statements are true

a) When we are valuating open items without update for reversal of the adjustment posting after key date, key user can define another posting date in place of keydate + 1
b) When we have regrouped the receivables/vendors, system carries out adjustment postings
c) Allocating costs to financial accounting through external settlement, the G/L is updated online/real time

(More than one answer correct)

Answer – a, b, c

Explanation:

In the period when the valuation is performed (as defined by the key date), a posting is made to adjust the overall receivables balance for the change in exchange rates. This posting is reversed in the next period to bring the balances back to the original position. A subsequent valuation or payment clearing is then based on the original posting. The adjustment posting is carried out on the key date as usual, and then reversed on the following day. The user can however define another posting date.

Re grouping receivables / vendors system carries out adjustment postings.

Allocating costs to financial accounting through external settlement, the G/L is updated online/real time

3) Which of the following are special G/L types? Choose the correct answer(s)

a) Noted items
b) Down payments
c) Automatic offsetting entries (statistical)
d) Free offsetting entries
e) Other types

(More than one answer is correct)

Answer – a, c, d

Explanation:

Special G/L types are noted items, automatic offsetting entries and free offsetting entries. Special G/L transactions are transactions in the accounts receivable and payable, which are displayed separately in the general ledger and the sub ledgers

Down payments are not special GL transactions. The special G/L account (alternative reconciliation account) for down payments made is displayed on the financial statements in the payables area.

4) The following applies to the special general ledger type of noted items. Choose the correct answer(s)

a) The special G/L indicators of your own can be created of this type
b) The account for the offsetting entry is selected automatically
c) No postings are made on an offsetting account
d) Noted items are posted on an alternative reconciliation account
e) Noted items cannot replace any proper FI documents

(More than one answer correct)

Answer – c, d, e

Explanation:

Special G/L indicators for noted items can only be created as are individual account assignments. The account for the offsetting entry needs to be maintained in the configuration.

Automatic offsetting entries (statistical) are always made on the same offsetting account. To simplify the posting procedure, the number of the account for the offsetting entry is defined in Customizing.

Only one line item is updated if a noted item is created. No offsetting entry is made. That is why no zero balance check is made.
Noted items are posted on an alternative reconciliation account and this is maintained in customization. The alternative reconciliation account is specified in the target account and the base reconciliation is the normal customer/vendor reconciliation account.

Noted items are individual account assignments which are only used to remind the respective department of due payments or payments to be made and are not intended to be displayed in the general ledger and therefore cannot be considered as a FI document.

5) Which of the following are part of financial statements?

a) Automatic offsetting entries

b) Noted items
c) Free offsetting entries
d) All of the above

(Only one answer is correct)

Answer – c

Explanation:

Free offsetting entries are part of the financial statements. They are postings with freely definable offsetting entries.

Automatic offsetting entries (statistical) are transactions which are always posted on the same offsetting account. They are usually included in the notes to financial statements.

Noted items are individual account assignments which are only used to remind the respective department of due payments or payments to be made and are not intended to be displayed in the general ledger

6) Find the correct statement with respect to the Special G/L transactions.

a) Special G/L transactions can be divided into four classes
b) If sub-ledger account assignments are made using a special G/L indicator, the postings are performed on reconciliation account
c) The processing of down payments is integrated only in the payment programs.
d) It is possible to pass on documents for individual items to a reconciliation account using the special main ledger indicator.

(Only one answer is correct)

Answer – d

Explanation

Special G/L transactions can be divided in the three classes. (down payments, bill of exchange & other transactions)
If sub-ledger account assignments are made using a special G/L indicator, the postings are performed on an alternate reconciliation account.
The processing of down payments is integrated in the payment programs and in dunning.

7) Find the correct statements with respect to the Special General Ledger Types.

a) Automatic offsetting entries are transactions which are posted to different offsetting accounts.
b) Noted items are individual account assignments which are used to track the due payments or payments to be made and are not intended to be displayed in the General Ledger.
c) Special General Ledger type posting can be a free G/L account posting, a noted item or a posting with automatic offsetting entry.
d) Posting of a guarantee of payment is an example of a noted item.

(More than one answer correct)

Answer – b, c

Explanation

Automatic offsetting entries are transactions which are posted to the same setting account.
Posting of a guarantee of payment is an example of automatic offsetting entries.

8) Which statements describe the characteristics of the Automatic Offsetting entries?

a) Guarantees received are generally displayed in the financial statements.

b) These transactions are called statistical postings, since they are generally not displayed at all in the financial statements or are only displayed in the notes to the financial statements.
c) Several offsetting account numbers can be defined in Customizing.
d) If you clear open items in the respective accounts, the system automatically clears the respective items in the offsetting account.

(More than one answer correct)

Answer – a, b, d

Explanation

Only one offsetting account number can be defined in customizing.

9) Noted items

a) Perform a zero balance check at the time of processing the entry
b) Do not update the general ledger
c) Are administered as open items in accounts payable/receivable and special G/L accounts
d) Can be made as several line items at the time of creation

(More than one answer correct)

Answer – b, c

Explanation

Only one line item is updated if a noted item is created. No offsetting entry is made. Therefore no zero balance check is made.
Noted items can be created as a single line item at the time of creation

10) Find the correct sequence of a down payment in the customer area.

a) Down payment received→ Down payment request →Customer invoice →Clearing → Posting the down payment clearing with the invoice
b) Down payment received → Down payment request → Customer invoice → Posting the down payment clearing with the invoice → Clearing
c) Down payment request → Down payment received →Customer invoice →Clearing → Posting the down payment clearing with the invoice
d) Down payment request → Down payment received → Customer invoice → Posting the down payment clearing with the invoice → Clearing

(Only one answer is correct)

Answer – d

Explanation

Sequence of a down payment in customer area is as follows:

Down payment request: Down payment requests are noted items. They do not change any account balances. With down payment requests you can automatically issue dunning notices and make payments.

Down payment received: Received down payments are displayed as payables on your accounts. They may not change the balance of the "Receivables" reconciliation account. Received down payments are administered in the "Down Payments Received" alternative reconciliation account in the Payables area on the financial statements.
Customer invoice: The customer receives an invoice whenever goods are supplied or services performed.

Posting a down payment clearing with invoice: At this point of time the down payment is no longer a down payment. The amount should/must be displayed as payment on the normal reconciliation account.

Clearing of the items during the payment of the customer's balance

11) Which statements are correct with respect to setting up Special G/L transactions?

a) Special G/L transactions are posted from the application side by means of special
b) Posting keys using special G/L indicators.
c) The standard posting keys to post a Special G/L transaction are 09, 19, 29 and 39.
d) Special G/L transactions are posted to an alternate G/L account stored in Customizing.
e) The alternative reconciliation account type (D/K) is defined in the company code segment of the G/L master record.

(More than one answer correct)

Answer – a, b, c, d

Explanation

Posting keys 09, 19, 29 & 39 are used to enter special G/L indicators. Alternative reconciliation account is specified in the customization. This is always tagged to a reconciliation account.

12) What area the similarities between a normal reconciliation account and an alternative reconciliation account?

a) Definition of the account type (customer/vendor) in the GL master
b) Line item display is always activated for both
c) Posting keys used to post the transactions are similar
d) Direct postings to both these accounts are not possible

(More than one answer correct)

Answer – a, d

Explanation

Line items, if activated, display for alternative reconciliation accounts. Line item display is not always activated for normal reconciliation accounts.
Different posting keys are used for both transactions.
Posting keys 09, 19, 29 and 39 are used to enter special G/L transactions.
Normal Customer/vendor posting keys can be used to enter transactions for a normal reconciliation account.

13) What are the characteristics of a Special G/L indicator?

a) These transactions are not relevant to credit check
b) Only certain posting keys can be used with the respective special G/L indicators.
c) Warnings against commitments can be activated.
d) Special G/L transaction class is the same for a down payment, a bill of exchange or any other type

(More than one answer correct)

Answer – b, c

Explanation

You can include special G/L transactions in the credit limit check for customers. Noted items are generally not taken into account. All other transactions can be marked accordingly as desired by the user.
The special G/L transaction class determines whether the transaction is a down payment, a bill of exchange or any other type of transaction.

14) Which of the following transactions needs to be routed through a Special G/L indicator?

a) An advance payment to a supplier
b) Advance received from a customer
c) A foreign currency customer invoice
d) Advance to a one-time vendor

(More than one answer correct)

Answer – a, b

Explanation

A foreign currency invoice can be entered in the similar manner to a local customer invoice. This transaction does not need to go through a special G/L indicator. Advances cannot be given to one-time vendors.

15) Which statement is correct with respect to postings through special G/L indicators?

a) The main reconciliation account in the vendor/customer master gets updated
b) The alternative reconciliation account in the vendor/customer master gets updated
c) The alternative reconciliation account mapped to the main reconciliation account of the vendor/customer gets updated
d) Both alternative reconciliation account and the main reconciliation account get updated

(Only one answer correct)

Answer – c

Explanation

Postings through special G/L indicators do not update the main reconciliation account in the customer/vendor master records. It only updates the alternative reconciliation account mapped to the main reconciliation account of the vendor/customer record.

Parking Documents

1) Which data of a parked document can be changed?

a) Currency
b) Posting date
c) Document type
d) Account assignment objects

(More than one answer correct)

Answer – b, d

Explanation

Document currency and the Document type of a parked document cannot be changed.

2) Find the correct statements with respect to document parking?

a) You can only park documents for customer accounts and vendor accounts.
b) A number of header and item fields can be edited in a parked document.
c) A customer invoice can be parked by an accounts clerk and a workflow message can be sent automatically to the supervisor for approval.
d) You can enter and store incomplete documents in SAP without having to check the entries extensively by parking the documents

(More than one answer correct)

Answer – b, c, d

Explanation

You can park documents for customer accounts, vendor accounts and G/L accounts.

3) What happens when a parked document is turned into a "proper" document?

a) A new document number is generated.
b) The transaction figures are updated.
c) History (e.g. changes to parked documents) is documented
d) All answers above are correct

(More than one answer correct)

Answer – b, c

Explanation

The document number remains the same.

4) Find the incorrect statements with respect to document parking.

a) Document deletion is possible for both parked documents as well as posted documents.
b) Parked documents do not update the transaction figures while posted documents update the transaction figures
c) Certain fields can be amended for both parked and posted documents
d) The amount can be changed in both parked and posted documents

(More than one answers incorrect)

Answer – a, d

Explanation

Document deletion is possible for parked documents. Once a document is posted it is not possible to delete. But this document can be reversed. Amount can be changed for park documents but once a document is posted, the amount cannot be changed

5) Find the characteristics of a held document?

a) Do not update the transaction figures
b) Document number is assigned
c) These documents are not taken in to reports
d) All statements are correct

(More than one answer correct)

Answer – a, c

Explanation

A document number is not assigned to a held document.

6) When a document is parked

a) The actual document number is generated but the document is not posted
b) A temporary document number is generated but the document is not posted
c) The document is posted with the actual document number
d) The document is posted with a temporary document number account number

(Only one answer correct)

Answer – a

Explanation

When a document is parked the document number is generated based on the selected document type. But transaction figures will not get updated.

7) A parked document can be

a) Modified
b) Posted
c) Deleted
d) All of the above

(Only one answer correct)

Answer – d

Explanation

Certain fields in both the document header and line items can be modified: eg: Posting date and document date, Cost assignment obect, account and amount. A parked document can either be posted or deleted after checking the accuracy.

8) Document parking is used:

a) to process the documents faster
b) to hold the documents for the new session
c) for subsequently completing and posting incomplete documents
d) None of the above

Which of the above statements are correct?
(Only one answer is correct)

Answer – c

Explanation

Parked documents can be supplemented, checked and posted later on – if necessary, by a different operator. No data, such as transaction figures can be updated when parking documents. The data of parked documents is available to the system for real-time evaluations. In this way, amounts from parked documents can be used for example for the advance return for tax on sales/purchases. The Park Document function is available for conventional postings and the Enjoy Posting Mask.

9) The following statements refer to document parking

1. **Changes to parked documents can be only displayed after posting the document**
2. **Dates, amounts, accounts and cost center assignments can be changed in a parked document**
3. **The document change rules stored for posted documents in the system are not applied to parked documents.**
4. **A batch input session can be created in order to post parked documents.**

Which of the following is correct with respect to the above statements?

a) 1and 2 are correct
b) Only2 and 3 are correct

c) 2, 3 and 4 are correct
d) all of the above are correct

(Only one answer is correct)

Answer – c

Explanation

Changes to parked documents can be displayed before or after posting them.

10) The following are fields in a parked document.

1. **Document Currency**
2. **Document number**
3. **Document Type**
4. **Company code**

Identify the fields which cannot be modified.

a) only 1 and 2
b) only 3 and 4
c) 1, 2 and 4
d) all of the above

(Only one answer is correct)

Answer – d

Explanation

All of the above fields cannot be modified once a document is parked.

11) Identify the fields which can be modified in a parked document

a) Posting date and document date
b) GL account, Customer account and vendor account
c) Account assignment objects
d) Amounts in the document

(More than one answer is correct)

Answer – a, b, c, d

Explanation

You can edit parked documents and also complete them step-by-step. A number of header and item fields can be edited, including the amounts. The document change rules stored for documents posted in the system are not applied to parking documents! The currency, the document type/number and the company code cannot be changed. Multiple changes are also possible. Dates, amounts, accounts and account assignment objects can be changed. Changes can be made to individual documents, individual items, to several documents by means of lists or with the line item list.

Validations/Substitutions

1) Which scenarios can be managed by introducing a substitution rule?

a) To default the cost center for a particular GL account.
b) To generate a error message if a different document type is entered
c) To default the business area for an accounting document
d) All of the above

(More than one answers correct)

Answer – a, c

Explanation:

A validation rule needs to be created to generate an error message if a different document type is entered.

2) Find the correct statements with respect to substitution & validation.

a) A validation/substitution can be valid only for one company code at a given time
b) Only one validation/substitution can be activated for one company code for a call-up point
c) Validation/substitution for the correct call-up point must be activated.
d) Two call-up points have been provided for a finance document.

(More than one answer is correct)

Answer – b, c

Explanation:

A validation/substitution can be valid for several company codes at the same time. Three call-up points have been provided for a finance document. (Document header/document line/complete document)

Archiving FI

1) Name reasons for archiving data

a) Improve response times
b) Keep data secret from auditors
c) Reduce system downtimes during software upgrades
d) Lower the effort involved in database administration

(More than one answer is correct)

Answer – a, c, d

Explanation:

A large data volume can lead to performance bottlenecks that cause poor performance on the user side and increased consumption of resources on the administration side. Therefore, data that is no longer required from the perspective of applications can be removed from the database. Simply deleting the data, however, is not an option since read access to the data may still be required. Therefore, the data must be transferred from the database to external storage media so that it can be read later.

The data archiving function enables you to remove mass data from the database that is no longer needed in the system but which must still be stored so that it can be analyzed. The procedures, execution times and so on for archiving data in Financial Accounting are specified according to applicable regulations

2) Why should data be archived? Find the correct reasons.

a) Lower the effort for database administration
b) To accommodate country specific storage regulations
c) Reduce the system downtime for software upgrades, recoveries and database backups
d) All of the above

(Only one answer is correct)

Answer – d

Explanation:

The data archiving function enables you to remove mass data from the database that is no longer needed in the system however, which must still be stored so that it can be analyzed. Depending on country, there are different regulations governing how long documents, master data, and so on must be retained in systems.

3) An archiving object is basically made up of how many components?

a) 1
b) 2
c) 3
d) 4

(Only one answer is correct)

Answer – c

Explanation:

An archiving object is basically made up of three components: data declaration part/ Customizing settings/programs.
The data declaration part describes all the relevant database objects that characterize an application object. The customizing settings are used to set archiving object-specific parameters for an archiving procedure.

4) Information provided by the archiving monitor includes

a) Summarized information about the individual archiving procedures
b) Progress bars while processing archive files
c) Open alerts
d) All of the above

(More than one answer is correct)

Answer – b, c

Explanation:

Archiving monitor includes detailed information about the individual archiving procedures.

5) Out of the following which gets checked during the archiving procedure?

a) All entries have been cleared for open item managed accounts
b) Open purchase orders for the period
c) Fiscal years to be archived contain any periods that are still open for posting
d) G/L account has a deletion indicator

(More than one answer is correct)

Answer – a, b, c, d

Explanation:

Archiving Logic things checked during the archiving procedure		
for transaction figures	**for master data**	**for documents**

- Do the fiscal years to be archived contain any periods that are still open for posting?	**Banks:** - Has a deletion indicator been set? - Is the bank no longer being used? **G/L accounts:** - Has a deletion indicator been set? - Are there (still) transaction figures (e.g. have they already been archived)? - Are there (still) documents? **Customers/vendors** - Has a deletion indicator been set? - Are there (still) transaction figures (e.g. have they already been archived)? - Are there (still) documents?	- Has the document type run time been maintained? - Has the account run time been maintained? - Are the items cleared in the case of open item-managed accounts?

6) What are the characteristics in the document header which should get fulfilled in archiving procedure?

a) Recurring, parked or sample documents are taken into consideration
b) Document with a withholding tax remain in the system for at least 455 days.
c) The document must have been in the system for longer than the minimum number of days (minimum duration).
d) All of the above

(More than one answer is correct)

Answer – b, c

Explanation:

Recurring, parked or sample documents are not taken into consideration for archiving procedure.

New General Ledger

1) How many possibilities are possible with New General Ledger? Choose all that apply

a) Account balancing with any characteristic
b) Customer Fields Extensibility
c) Segment Reporting
d) Reduction of Total Cost of Ownership
e) Transparency and Uniformity

(More than one answer is correct)

Answer – a, b, c, d, e

Explanation:

Possibilities of the new general ledger are as follows:

- The user can enter user-defined fields and update the relevant totals: Customer fields extensibility
- The end user no longer has to carry out time-consuming reconciliation tasks between FI and CO for the end of period since cross-entity processes are transferred in real-time to the new General Ledger in Controlling. Furthermore, you can, for example, navigate from the financial statements report results or the profit and loss statement report results to the relevant CO report. This reduces the total cost of ownership.
- Due to the new 'multi-dimensional' aspect in the General Ledger, all data that is relevant for the General Ledger is stored in one environment. As a result, reconciliation tasks, for example, between the general ledger and Profit Center Accounting or the consolidation staging ledger, and processing steps that have to be carried out repeatedly in the individual applications (for example, balance carry forward) are no longer required. When you use the new General Ledger, you may not have to use the special ledger anymore. : Account balancing with any characteristic & transparency and uniformity
- The 'Segment' entity and the relevant reporting that are required for segment reporting according to IAS and U.S. GAAP are available in the new General Ledger. : Segment reporting

2) The New General Ledger now consists of what functions? Choose all that apply.

a) FI Classic
b) Profit Center Accounting
c) Product Costing
d) Reconciliation Ledger
e) Schedule Manager

(More than one answer is correct)

Answer – a, d

Explanation:

The New G/L merges the classic general ledger with profit center accounting, special ledgers (including cost-of sales ledger), and the consolidation-staging ledger.

Also, New G/L uses a broad, unified data basis, so that G/L account, functional area, and profit center are contained in a single data record. This enhances data quality and eliminates the need for reconciliation measures in the reconciliation ledger (previously, the reconciliation ledger had to be used to reconcile CO with FI).

Profit center accounting, product costing and schedule manager are functionalities available even in the older versions.

3) What are the advantages of using the New General Ledger? Choose all that apply.

a) Extended data structure
b) Document (Online) Split
c) Real Time Integration between CO and FI
d) Multiple Ledgers can be maintained under leading ledger.
e) Interfaces for entering the data and postings are nearly identical.

Answer – All of the above

Explanation:

Extended data structure allows the use of different ledgers based on the customer reporting needs.
Document splitting allows you to display documents using a differentiated representation. In the representation, line items are split according to selected dimensions. In this way, you can draw up complete financial statements for the selected dimensions at any time.
The real time integration between CO and FI enables faster reconciliation between ledgers.
Multiple ledgers can be maintained under the leading ledger.
Information which flows from interfaces and data entry is identical in most if the instance.

4) True or False: Please choose the correct answer.

a) The New GL is optional for existing SAP Customers. True / False
b) New SAP customers will have to activate New GL by Default. True / False
c) ECC 6.0 will prohibit the use of PCA above General Ledger. True / False
d) The new SAP Installation will choose between Old and New Ledger. True / False
e) Customers within New Ledger will have limited extensibility. True / False

(Only one answer is correct)

Answer – a is True all others are False

Explanation: It is optional for the existing customers to activate the new GL function. . Even new customers need not activate the New G/L.

5) What Customizing transaction will activate the New General Ledger? Choose all that apply.

a) FANEWGL_ACTIVATION
b) FAGL_ACTIVATION
c) GL_ACTIVATION
d) NEWGL_ACTIVATION
e) FIGL_ACTIVATION

(Only one answer correct)

Answer – b

Explanation:

To make the settings and use the functions in General Ledger Accounting, you have to activate it. To do this, in Customizing choose Financial Accounting→ Financial Accounting Global Settings→ Activate New General Ledger Accounting (FAGL_ACTIVATION)

6) After Activating the New GL, what following changes will take place? Choose all that apply.

a) There will be new Paths for New GL in addition to existing (Old) GL.
b) Conventional Financial Accounting Paths will remain at their present form.
c) Old paths can be eliminated by running RFAGL_SWAP_IMG_OLD
d) Old paths can be eliminated by running FIGL_SWAP_IMG_NEW

(More than one answer is correct)

Answer – a, b. c

Explanation:

Activating New General Ledger Accounting will establish new paths Running RFAGL_SWAP_IMG_OLD will hide the classic Financial Accounting paths. Running FIGL_SWAP_IMG_NEW will eliminate old paths.

7) What will be the new ledger definitions after the activation? Choose all that apply.

a) Control Parameters (as before) will be from company code.
b) The leading ledger will manage local currency(s) assigned to company code.
c) New GL will use the same Fiscal Year Variant and Posting Period Variant that is assigned to company code.
d) There will be or can be multiple leading ledgers.
e) If multiple ledgers are used, values from all the ledgers can be posted on to CO.

(More than one answer is correct)

Answer – a, b, c

Explanation:

Control parameters after activating the new general ledger continue to be from company code. Local currency is also managed by the company code. The assignment of the fiscal year variant and the posting period variant and the to the leading ledger is located in IMG → Financial accounting →Financial accounting global setting →Ledgers →Fiscal year and posting periods.

There can be only one leading ledger.
If multiple ledgers are used, values from all the leading ledgers are posted on to CO.

8) Choose the correct answer(s).

a) After activation, Financial Accounting Document will have two views: the entry
view and the GL View.
True / False

b) Entry View will be the same in sub-ledgers (AR / AR / AA / Taxes).
True / False

c) The way the document will appear in General Ledger view will be the same as
Entry view.
True / False

d) There will be no extra views on documents and no changes will be made.
True / False

(More than one answer is correct)

Answer – a, b, d are True. c is False.

Explanation:

In General Ledger Accounting, you can display documents that have already been posted in the entry view or, for a ledger, in the general ledger view:

- Entry View - In the entry view, a document contains the document line items originally entered or transferred from the original component. If you choose document display, the document is first displayed in the entry view.

- General Ledger View - In the general ledger view, a document contains the document line items originally entered or transferred from the original component, split line items generated by document splitting, or additionally generated clearing items. Documents in the general ledger view always apply to a specific ledger.

9) Accounts are determined using 'derivation rules' consisting the following. Which of them is/are optional?

a) Source fields
b) Target fields
c) Conditions
d) Rule entries

(Only one answer is correct)

Answer – c

Explanation:

Accounts are determined using derivation rules. These rules consist of:

- Conditions under which the derivation rule is executed (optional)
- Determination of fields used in the derivation rule here you define. Source fields (derivation rule input) all fields filled from the Accrual Engine.
- Target fields (derivation rule output) all fields that must be filled for successful account determination, or user-defined parameters that you can use for sequential derivation rules.
- The rule entries themselves that derive the input for the target fields from the content of the source fields.

10) Which of the following are advantages of document splitting?

a) Accelerate closing
b) Increased data quality
c) Extensibility and flexibility
d) Real-time integration

(More than one answer is correct)

Answer – a, b, c

Explanation:

New G/L uses a broad, unified data basis, so that G/L account, functional area, and profit center are contained in a single data record. This enhances data quality and obviates the need for reconciliation measures (previously, the reconciliation ledger had to be used to reconcile CO with FI). The period-end closing now can be completed more quickly. Thus, using New G/L removes the need to use several separate components.
Real time integration is achieved through the use of leading/non leading ledgers.

11) Which of the following are advantages of ledger solution?

a) You maintain a separate ledger for every accounting principle
b) You can use different fiscal year variants in this scenario
c) The number of G/L accounts is manageable
d) The data volume decreases

(More than one answer is correct)

Answer – a, b, c

Explanation:

Separate accounting principles are used for different ledgers. Eg: Balance sheet items and P & L account balances are stored in different table structures/ledgers.
Different fiscal years can be maintained in the same instance. But when assigning to a controlling area the fiscal year and the controlling area must be in the same fiscal year.
Number of GL accounts can be managed by the use of different options like the transaction type and Reference Key fields.
Data volumes do not decrease by using different ledgers.

12) When planning statistical key figures, it uses a ________________ for period-based distribution of the total values. Please select the option that fulfills the above statement

a) receiver base
b) free entry
c) planned value
d) distribution key
e) secondary statistical key figure

(Only one answer is correct)

Answer – d

Explanation:

Period based distribution is carried over from the period in which it is entered up to all subsequent periods of the same fiscal year. This is done through a distribution key during the statistical key figure planning.

13) Plan values on cost centers can often be calculated using mathematical dependencies.
__________________ let's you use calculation dependencies to plan your cost center costs.
Please select the option that fulfills the above statement:

a) formula planning
b) resource planning
c) dependency planning
d) accrual calculation
e) distribution

(Only one answer is correct)

Answer – a

Explanation:

Formula planning lets you use calculation dependencies to plan your cost center costs. You can define these dependencies as formulas in templates that are independent of the cost center. In this way, cost centers with similar templates can use the same formulas.

You can use the following data from the SAP R/3 System in formula planning:

- All master data information for the cost center, for example, to define constraints.
- All master data information for the activity type, for example, to define constraints.
- Any primary planned costs
- Plan activity, scheduled activity and capacity for any cost center/activity type
- Any statistical key figures

14) Consider the following statements about Report Painter:

1. **____<1>____ are numeric fields that you can evaluate in a report.**
2. **____<2>____ are fields that display criteria that you used in the data selection.**

3. **____<3>____ consist of a key figure and one or more characteristics.**
4. **All of the reports are kept in ____<4>____.**

Please choose the option that substitutes <1>, <2>, <3> and <4>, respectively:

a) key figures, predefined columns, system libraries and characteristics
b) predefined columns, key figures, system libraries and characteristics
c) predefined columns, characteristics, key figures, and system libraries
d) key figures, characteristics, predefined columns and system libraries
e) characteristics, key figures, predefined columns and system libraries

(Only one answer is correct)

Answer – d

Explanation:

A key figure performs various cell calculations within a report, such as subtracting subtotals within a column. The key figure pinpoints particular locations of a key figure block within the column-row matrices of a report.
A characteristic is a single field or column of a database table that display the criteria that you used in the data selection.
Pre-defined columns consist of a key figure and one or more characteristics
All report painter reports are saved in the system libraries.

15) Consider the following sentences and choose the correct option:

a) All transactions carried out during a period are stored with a date weighting in the average balance ledger.
b) The opening balance is taken from the average balance ledger "8A".
c) The average balance ledger (8Z) contains both weighted transactions by period and by
company code.

d) A transfer price is a price used to plan the transfer of goods and services that should be
occur between independent organizational units.
e) The assignment of a Report Painter/Report Writer to a library is optional.

(Only one answer is correct)

Answer – a

Explanation:

You can store average balances for actual data by period and profit center using a separate ledger in Profit Center Accounting using the average balance ledger.

Ledger 8A is used for management and segment reporting, and other special ledgers for multi-dimensional, customer-specific requirements.

8Z ledger is used to activate or deactivate an average balance ledger for Profit Center Accounting. The system automatically creates a fixed ledger "8Z" for the summary record table in Profit Center Accounting. (Table GLPCT).

Transfer prices let organizations that divide tasks among different organizational units to valuate the goods and services exchanged between these units.

The assignment of a Report Painter/Report Writer to a library is mandatory.

16) Which program hides the old paths in the new general ledger

a) FANEWGL_ACTIVATION
b) RFAGL_SWAP_IMG_OLD
c) FANEWGL _SWAP_IMG_OLD
d) RFIGL_SWAP_IMG_OLD

(Only one answer is correct)

Answer – b

Explanation:

RFAGL_SWAP_IMG_OLD : Activate/Deactivate Old Implementation paths in the new GL

Assessment/Distribution/Reposting

1) Consider the following statements:

1. Reposting line items creates CO documents which don't contain a reference to the FI document.
2. Commitments are payment obligations that are not entered into the accounts, but that
   lead to actual costs at a later date.
3. Purchase orders reduce the commitment values.
4. To directly allocate activity, create an activity type of the category 1 (manual entry,
   manual allocation).
5. You can reposting direcy activity allocations in periods and in the same period from
   which the document to be adjusted originates.

Choose the correct option:

a) 1 and 5 are correct
b) 2 and 3 are correct
c) 2 and 4 are correct
d) 1 and 3 are correct
e) 4 and 5 are correct

(Only one answer is correct)

Answer – c

Explanation:

You can manually repost primary costs and revenues using event-based reposting's. You use this function mainly to adjust (correct) posting errors. When you make an internal reposting, the primary costs are reposted (under the original cost element) to

a receiving order. It also reduces the commitment values if any. Commitments are payment obligations that are not entered into the accounts, but that
lead to actual costs at a later date.
Reposting line items creates CO documents which will contain a reference to the FI document
You cannot repost directly activity allocations in periods and in the same period form which the document to be adjusted originates.

2) Which of the following are correct about periodic allocation?

a) Both Distribution & Assessment can be applied as a Periodic Allocation Technique in the
New Ledger. However Periodic Reposting is not used.
b) Statistical Key Figure presently cannot be used as a Tracing Factor.
c) Distribution Generates a FI Document as an output.
d) A separate Assessment account needs to be defined for New General Ledger as a GL Account that is not a secondary Cost Element of category.

(More than one answer is correct)

Answer – All of the above

Explanation:

You can only use periodic reposting and distribution for primary cost elements. The costs are transferred to the receivers using the original cost element, so they are transferred to the primary cost elements of the receiver.
Statistical Key Figures can be used as a tracing factor.
The assessment allocates primary as well as secondary costs. The information on the original primary cost elements for the sender is lost because the costs are allocated using an assessment cost element (category 42). You can use more than one assessment cost element for differentiation purposes. Distribution generates a FI document.

3) Which of the following statements are true (Please choose the correct option(s))?

a) The SAP R/3 system saves the information from the clearing cost center in totals records
during a periodic reposting.
b) The cycle-segment method is used only for defining periodic reposting.
c) Independent cycles can be processed in parallel if they have the same allocation type.
d) You can process cycles in the same cycle flow group in parallel.

e) During distribution, the original cost elements are summarized into distribution cost
elements (secondary cost element category = 42).

(Only one answer is correct)

Answer – c

Explanation:

The SAP system does not save the information from the clearing cost center in totals records during a periodic reposting. This enables the SAP system to save memory when storing the data records. Several segments are grouped together in one cycle. You can only repost primary costs. During this process, the original cost element remains the same.
Cycle method can be used for reposting as well as assessment and distribution. They can be processed in parallel only if they have the same allocation type.
Line items are posted for the sender as well as for the receiver, enabling the allocation to be recorded in detail
During distribution, the original cost elements are not summarized into distribution cost elements

Workflow

1) Which statements are correct?

a) A company code can be assigned several workflow variants
b) A task can be assigned one possible processor only
c) It is possible to design multilevel workflow sequences
d) The same workflow variant can be assigned to several company codes.

(More than one answer correct)

Answer – c, d

Explanation:

Several company codes can be assigned to the workflow variants. However, a company code cannot be assigned several workflow variants.
A task can be assigned to more than one processor.
One workflow variant can be used for several company codes. It is possible to create multilevel workflow sequences. Individual tasks can usually be assigned several possible processors.

2) Which of the following are process dimensions of SAP business workflow?

a) Organizational structure
b) Process structure
c) Function
d) Information

(More than one answer correct)

Answer – all of the above

Explanation:

In the SAP business workflow, the four process dimensions:

- Organizational structure (Who?)
- Process structure (When? In what order? Under what circumstances?)
- Function (What?)
- Information (With what data?)

3) Which of the following are screen areas of Business Workplace?

a) Selection tree
b) Workflow
c) Worklist
d) Work item preview

(More than one answer is correct)

Answer – a, c, d

Explanation:

The Business Workplace consists of three screen areas:

Selection tree: You can find the selection tree on the left side of the Business Workplace. Here you can select work items to be executed, workflows which you have started or documents.

Worklist: The worklist is displayed at the top right of the Business-Workplace screen in case you want to mark the "Workflow" folder. The system automatically puts the entries in groups in this folder. There are special folders in which you can find overdue work items or missed deadline work items. If you mark "Inbox" in the selection tree, you can see all work items and documents in this area of the screen.

Work item preview: The work item selected from the work list is displayed in a preview at the bottom right of the screen. Not all functions of the work item display or workflow log are available. It is possible for the user to make a decision from within the work item preview

4) Which statements correctly describe the work flow in SAP?

a) Work flow co-ordinates certain integrated tasks
b) It is not tied to a particular application and can be adopted to customer requirements
c) Works the same way in all applications

d) Is a tool for the automation of business processes in SAP systems and between other systems

(More than one answer is correct)

Answer: b, c, d

Explanation:

SAP workflows co-ordinates with all integrated tasks.

5) Identify the correct examples of SAP workflow.

a) Early archiving can be activated through document management workflows
b) Escalation procedures can be maintained through exception handling workflows
c) Purchase requisitions and travel requests can be maintained through approval workflows
d) All of the above are correct

(More than one answer is correct)

Answer – a, c

Explanation:

Escalation procedures can be maintained through deadline monitoring workflows. Purchase requisitions, invoice parking and travel requests can be maintained through approval workflows.

6) Identify the correct statements with respect to work flow in SAP.

a) Business work-flow consists of three screen areas namely selection tree, work list and work item preview.
b) The Web-flow engine determines the recipients of the work item. All selected recipients can view the work item and perform it at their Business Workplace.
c) Several users can perform the work items.
d) More than one company code can be assigned to work-flow variants.
e) It is not possible to apply different release procedures to different accounts receivable and payables.

(More than one answer is correct)

Answer – a

Explanation:

The Web-flow Engine determines the recipients of the work item. All selected recipients can view the work item and perform it at their Business Workplace. However, only one user can perform the work item. If a user starts to perform the work item, the other recipients are unable to execute this work item. A recipient can accept a work item. An accepted work item can only be performed by the user who has accepted it. It is possible to apply different release procedures to different accounts receivable and payables. This can be controlled by means of the release group field in the accounts receivable and accounts payable masters.

Planning

1) **What can we say about Planner Profile (Note: we can have more than one correct sentence. Please select the sentences you think they are correct)?**

   a) It allows to control the planning process.
   b) In a given planner profile, you cannot assign any number of planning layouts to any number of planning areas.
   c) The R/3 system contains standard planner profiles.
   d) Planner profiles are defined using the Report Painter.
   e) You can assign more than one planning layout to each planning area in the planning
   profile.

   (More than one answer correct)

Answer – a, c, e

Explanation:

Planner profile is a hierarchical structure containing planning layouts differentiated according to planning area. Each planning area uses one or more defined planning layouts.
You use planner profiles to control the way planning is carried out. System contains standard profiles too. New profiles can be created in the customizations.

2) **Consider the following statements (Plan Integration):**

   1. The____<1>____ is usually created to determine the quantities you expect to sell
   during the planning period.

   2. The ____<2>____ determines both the capacities and the quantity requirements for
   raw materials and operating supplies.

3. The ____<3>____ can be used to derive planning planned contribution margins.

4. The ____<4>____ is created once the activity units have been planned.

Please choose the option that substitutes <1>, <2>, <3> and <4>, respectively

a) sales plan, master production plan, cost plan , sales and profit plan
b) cost plan, sales plan, master production plan, sales and profit plan
c) sales plan, master production plan, cost plan, sales and profit plan
d) sales plan, sales and profit plan, master production plan, cost plan
e) sales plan, master production plan, sales and profit plan, cost plan
(Only one answer is correct)

Answer – e

Explanation:

Drawing up a valuated sales plan is a sub process of the company-wide, integrated planning process and is performed in Profitability Analysis. This will include the quantities you wish to sell during the planning period.
Production plan determines both the capacities and the quantity requirements for raw materials and operating supplies. This is derived from the sales plan.
Sales and profit plans can be used to derive planning planned contribution margins
Once the activity units have been planned, it is necessary to plan the costs expected for these activities. Cost center planning can thus be divided into planning the activity units and planning the expected costs incurred.

Schedule Manager

1) What are the functions integrated in the Schedule Manager (Note: we can have more than one correct sentence. Please select the sentences you think they are correct)?

a) Error correction and Restart
b) Various ways for starting jobs
c) Dependencies
d) Documentation integrated into the system
e) Uniform Error Analysis.

(More than one answer is correct)

Answer – a, c, d, e

Explanation:

Integrated functions in the Schedule Manager are:

- Uniform Error Analysis
- Uniform Start for Jobs
- Error Correction and Restart
- Dependencies
- Communication
- Documentation integrated into the system

The Schedule Manager does not facilitate different ways for starting jobs.

2) What are the advantages of using the Schedule Manager during the period-end closing processes (Note: we can have more than one correct sentence. Please select the sentences you think they are correct)?

a) Changes not recognized or active immediately
b) Changes are immediately visible and effective
c) Access is available to everyone with authorization
d) The system executes settlement

e) Documentation and flow for period-end closing are centrally integrated in the R/3 system

(More than one answer correct)

Answer – b, c, d, e

Explanation:

The Schedule Manager makes period-end closing easier and reflects a cross-application access point for all tasks involved in the closing process. It includes all steps, from defining the structure of your closing process, to scheduling the jobs and monitoring the results. You can use the Schedule Manager at any time to check when, and which activities are to be executed, and with which result. The Schedule Manager not only facilitates period-end closing, it is also useful in other components of the SAP System. It assists with the definition, scheduling, execution, and control of periodic tasks, and complex processes that have to be executed regularly.

3) What is the intention of a task list?

a) It is intended to group all work to be done
b) It is intended to be restricted to the financial manager
c) It is intended to make the user list the transaction codes
d) It is intended only to collect several jobs
e) It is intended to be self-documented

(Only one answer correct)

Answer – a

Explanation:

The Task List allows you to create tasks which you can assign to specific users. Your workflow may consist of multiple approval task requests and / or multiple action items. This will group all work to be done.

4) What are the four task types (Note: we can have more than one correct sentence)?

a) Create transaction code
b) Notes
c) Transactions
d) Programs with variant
e) Flow definition

(More than one answer correct)

Answer – b, c, d, e

Explanation:

The four task types in SAP are the notes, Transactions, Programs with variants and the flow definition.

5) What does the monitor provide (Note: we can have more than one correct sentence. Please select the sentences you think they are correct)?

a) The access to messages and result lists
b) The visualization of both entire technical and business information
c) The opportunity to postpone someone's tasks
d) The opportunity to view the work of colleagues and the processing sequence, as well as
the technical and business status of every task
e) The ability to monitor the total progress of period-end closing when the user uses more
than one task list

(More than one answer correct)

Answer – a, b, d, e

Explanation:

The monitor provides the call up detailed information on the active or completed jobs and flows that was scheduled in the scheduler. Some of the activities are:

- To access to messages and result lists.
- To visualization of both entire technical and business information
- To provide opportunity to view the work of colleagues and the processing sequence, as well as
  the technical and business status of every task.
- To provide the ability to monitor the total progress of period-end closing when the user uses more than one task list.

6) What do the flow definitions provide (Note: we can have more than one correct sentence. Please select the sentences you think they are correct)?

a) To define dependencies via external tools
b) To execute it only when the system is online

c) To define a fixed sequence of jobs that is integrated in the R/3 system
d) To allow the user a way for changing period-end closing data
e) To send mails to colleagues at defined times.

(More than one answer is correct)

Answer – c, e

Explanation:

A flow definition consists of individual flow steps. It is a graphical summary of several steps. These steps include scheduling programs with variants in the job control of the SAP System so that fixed sequences of jobs are integrated in the R/3 system, and interaction with users by email.

It cannot define dependencies via external tools and does not provide users a way of changing period – end closing data.

7) What does the Work list provide (Note: we can have more than one correct sentence. Please select the sentences you think they are correct)?

a) Each job reads the relevant objects from the database, validates and process the objects
and after, posts the results to the database. This leads to an unnecessary sequential of
database accesses.
b) A chain can contain between four and ten steps.
c) It is only after all jobs are run that the system detects any object errors that occurred
d) The selection report selects all objects from the database that are relevant for subsequent
jobs. The system creates a special place for every object
e) A chain can contain any number of jobs.

(More than one answer is correct)

Answer – d, e

Explanation:

Worklists are the quickest and most convenient way of accessing the objects that you need to translate. Worklists have a hierarchical structure that organizes the objects you need to translate under object types for translation (e.g. data elements, program texts, etc.), that are in turn organized according to object groups. The object groups are sorted according to priority in the worklist structure, enabling you to translate the most important object types (e.g. table entries, Customizing texts) first.

Worklist provides:

- The selection report selects all objects from the database that are relevant for subsequent
  jobs. The system creates a special place for every object.
- A chain can contain any number of jobs.

8) Which program hides the old paths in the new general ledger

a) FANEWGL_ACTIVATION
b) RFAGL_SWAP_IMG_OLD
c) FANEWGL _SWAP_IMG_OLD
d) RFIGL_SWAP_IMG_OLD

(Only one answer is correct)

Answer – b

Explanation:

RFAGL_SWAP_IMG_OLD : Activate/Deactivate Old Implementation paths in the new GL

9) What are the building blocks for the SAP Solution Management strategy (Please choose the correct option)?

a) Safeguarding Management, Empowering Management, Solution Management
Optimization, Support Programs Management and Testing Management.
b) Global Strategy and Service Level Management, Business Process Management,
Management of mySAP technology, Software Change Management and Support Desk
Management.
c) Project Management, Blueprint Definition Management, Configuration Management,
Customizing Synchronization Management and Testing Management.
d) Integrated Product Management, Project Monitoring and Control, Configuration
Management, Supplier Agreement Management and Organizational Effort Management.

e) Supply Chain Management, Customer Relationship Management, Strategic Enterprise
Management, Business Warehouse Management and Advanced Planner Optimizing.

(Only one answer is correct)

Answer – b

Explanation:

Solution Manager is a centralized support and system management suite. A SAP system landscape may include a large quantity of system installations of SAP systems. SAP Solution Manager tries to reduce and centralize the management of these systems. The building blocks of the solutions manager are:

- Global Strategy and Service Level Management
- Business Process Management
- Management of MySAP Technology
- Software Change Management
- Support Desk Management

10) SAP Solution Manager is (Note: we can have more than one correct sentence.
Please select the sentences you think they are correct):

a) A customer platform that enables representation and documentation of the entire SAP
documentation.

b) A platform that provides a single point of access into component systems for design,
configuration and testing activities.

c) A platform that provides with the Business Process Repository central access to the list of
predefined business scenarios, which serve as a starting point for identifying the project
scope to be implemented.

d) A platform that only enables component-oriented configuration and testing.

e) A platform that helps reducing the total costs of ownership (TCO).

(More than one answer is correct)

Answer – a, b, c, e

Explanation:

The SAP Solution Manager is the central platform for managing the mySAP Business Suite throughout its entire life cycle. It provides an extensive set of features in the IT Support area for enhancing, automating and improving the management of SAP systems.

SAP Solution Manager enables process-oriented versus component-oriented configuration and testing.
The SAP Solution Manager reduces your total cost of ownership and speeds up your return on investment in the solution landscape of your mySAP Business Suite by:

- Providing access to prepackaged business expertise in the form of methodology, documentation, and reliable preconfiguration for solutions of mySAP Business Suite, saving time and money and help you get to your solution on a fast and safe track.

- Improving project communication and therefore efficiency because everyone involved works in the same location.
- Ensuring that the documentation on your solution landscape is located centrally and is always up-to-date. This saves time, improves efficiency of system administration, and can avoid unnecessary investment.
- Alerting you proactively with real-time monitoring before problems become severe and can then only be solved at high cost with much manpower.
- Integrating message-solving functions of your support organization in the Support Desk. This simplifies the work of your staff and, if necessary, provides them with expert help from SAP Active Global Support.
- Serving as the single entry and delivery point for all SAP Support Services, so that you can improve performance, minimize downtime, increase user satisfaction and postpone hardware investments.

**11) What are the five phases of the Implementation Roadmap (Please choose the
correct option)?**

a) Global Strategy, Business Process Management of mySAP technology, Development
Management, Software Change Management and Support Desk Management.

b) Project Preparation, Business Blueprint, Realization, Final Preparation and Go Live &
Support.

c) Integrated Product Management, Project Monitoring and Control, Configuration
Management, Supplier Agreement Management and Organizational Effort Management.

d) Supply Chain Management, Customer Relationship Management, Strategic Enterprise

Management, Business Warehouse Management and Advanced Planner Optimizing.

e) Transactions, Logical Component, Documentation, IMG Assignments and Test Cases.

(Only one answer is correct)

Answer – b

Explanation:

The ASAP Roadmap provides the methodology for implementing and continuously optimizing your SAP System. It divides the implementation process into five phases and offers detailed Project Plans. The five stages of the methodology are Project Preparation, Business Blueprint, Realization, Final Preparation and Go Live & Support.

12) The SAP Solution Manager as the technical and operations infrastructure has some components. What are they (Please choose the correct option)?

a) Operations, Solution Monitoring and Support.
b) Schedule Manager, Solution Manager and Solution Monitor.
c) Transactions, Logical Component, Documentation, IMG Assignments and Test Cases.
d) Project Preparation, Business Blueprint, Realization, Final Preparation and Go Live & Support.
e) Workflow, SAP Notes search, SAP Notes assistant and interface to SAP Service Marketplace to send Support Notifications.

(Only one answer is correct)

Answer – a

Explanation:

The SAP Solution Manager supports you throughout the entire lifecycle of your solutions, from the Business Blueprint thru configuration to production operation. Operations, Solution Monitoring and Support are the technical and operations infrastructure components in solutions manager.

Miscellaneous/Reporting/Foreign Currency Valuation

1) Which of the following statements are true

a) A financial statement version consists of maximum 9 hierarchy levels
b) We cannot assign account group according to balance
c) Drill down reporting is a tool that enables to analyze sub-ledger transaction amount

Answer – all answers false

Explanation:

Financial statement version hierarchy depends on the complexity of the chart of accounts and the reporting structure. Account groups can be grouped according to the debit and credit balances separately. Drill down reporting is a tool to analyze the GL account balances/line items.

2) Foreign currency valuation is possible

a) Only for vendor/customer open items
b) Only balance sheet items (G/L items)
c) Both of the above

(Only one answer correct)

Answer – c

Explanation:

Foreign currency valuations are possible for all vendor/customer open items as well as balance sheet accounts in foreign currencies. In order to carry out a foreign currency valuation the valuation method, currency customizations and expense and revenue accounts for exchange rate differences from the valuation need to be configured. You must also specify balance sheet adjustment accounts for receivables and payables accounts. This can be done by accessing the OBA1 transaction.

3) We cannot select individual business transactions for locking from a list of all the actual and plan business transactions.
TRUE/FALSE

Answer – false

Explanation:

It is possible to copy actual values or plan values to a planning version for internal orders as well as for cost centers. The actual business transactions are assigned to the corresponding, manually-planned business transactions that can be manually planned locked.

4) Preclosing activities that begin in the old month include:

a) Open new accounting period
b) Foreign currency valuations and financial statement adjustments
c) Enter accruals/deferrals, process recurring entries and bad debt expense in AR, post depreciation and interest expenses in asset accounting
d) Creation of external and internal reports

(More than one answer is correct)

Answer – a, b, c, d

Explanation:

Pre-closing activities that begin in the old month include:

- Technical - Open new accounting period (FI), FI - Enter accruals/deferrals, process recurring entries and bad debt expense in AR, post depreciation and interest expenses in Asset Accounting
- MM - Maintain GR/IR clearing account, post material revaluations
- HR - Post payroll expenses
- SD - Post goods issues for deliveries to customers

- Technical - Close old month in (MM), close sub-ledgers (FI), preliminary close of G/L (FI)

5) Which of the following are "special items" in financial statement version?

a) Profit and loss results
b) Expenses
c) Accounts not assigned
d) Notes to financial statement

(More than one answer is correct)

Answer – a, c, d

Explanation:

Each financial statement version will have the following special items:
- Assets
- Liabilities
- Profit
- Loss
- Profit and loss results
- Accounts not assigned
- Notes to Financial Statement

6) Which of the following are required settings for foreign currency valuation

a) Define exchange rates
b) Define valuation methods
c) Define expense and revenue accounts for exchange rate differences
d) Specify balance sheet adjustment accounts for receivables and payables

(More than one answer is correct)

Answer – All of the above

Explanation:

In order to carry out a foreign currency valuation, following customization is required:

- Check the currency Customizing (for example, must have defined the exchange rates)
- Define valuation methods (for example, for the lowest value principle)
- Define expense and revenue accounts for exchange rate differences from the valuation. You must also specify balance sheet adjustment accounts for receivables and payables accounts.

7) The Accrual Engine can be used for the following purposes.

a) Lease accounting
b) Provisions for awards
c) Automatic accruals in financial accounting
d) Intellectual property management

(More than one answer is correct)

Answer – a, b, d

Explanation:

The Accrual Engine can be used for the following:

- Manual Accruals in Financial Accounting
- Provisions for Awards
- Lease Accounting
- Intellectual Property Management

Automatics accruals in financial accounting are carried out by generating RPTQTA00 report.

8) The following can be used for G/L account evaluations

a) Balance display
b) Key figure reports
c) Reports for financial statement analysis

d) Interim report

(More than one answer is correct)

Answer – a, b, c

Explanation:

The account balance display, key figure reports and financial statement analysis reports assist in the process of evaluating a G/L account. Interim reports cannot help with account evaluations.

9) What can you say about the standard hierarchy (Please choose the correct option)?

a) It is the top of a Profit Center group, which all Cost Centers/Profit Centers may be
assigned.
b) This is a representation of the board directors cost center.
c) It can be defined after creating cost centers.
d) It must be defined before creating cost centers.
e) Its name is defined after creating controlling area and it must follow certain SAP standard
rules, as having the same name of the Controlling Area.

(Only one answer is correct)

Answer – d

Explanation:

The standard hierarchy is an organizational structure of the cost centers. All cost centers within the controlling area must be assigned to the standard hierarchy. It must be defined before you can create cost centers. The name of the standard hierarchy can be specified at the time of creating the controlling area. All Profit/Cost centers must be assigned to the standard hierarchy.
Naming convention of the standard hierarchy is user defined.

10) Which of the following are Form Types in drilldown reporting?

a) Single axis form without key figure
b) Single axis form with key figure
c) Dual axis form with key figure
d) Dual axis form without key figure

(More than one answer is correct)

Answer – a, b, c

Explanation:

Reports using a single-axis Form with Key Figures - Here, the key figures (such as revenue, percentage of total) which appear in the rows within the form are determined. When defining the report, you choose the drilldown characteristics (e.g. branch, region).

In the drilldown list, the columns contain key figures, while the rows contain the values of the drilldown characteristics (here Illinois and New Jersey).
The detail list has only one column and contains the selected object (here Illinois) which you want to report on, while the rows contain the key figures.

In a single-axis form without key figures, characteristics are only selected in the columns. Using a formula, it is possible to define additional characteristics in the form (such as the variance as a difference between plan and actual). The characteristics selected in the form (such as plan/actual, plan/actual variance) determine which data is shown in the columns.

Reports using a two-axis Form with Key Figures
In the two-axis form with key figures, both the rows and the columns are defines with key figures or characteristics. These key figures can appear either in the rows or in the columns. If you choose to have the key figures in the rows, the characteristics appear in the columns.
When defining the report, you choose the drilldown characteristics as with other types of report.
In the two-axis form with key figures, both the rows and the columns are defines without any key figures or characteristics.

11) Which of the following is not a function of SAP List Viewer?

a) Select List.
b) Select Detail.
c) Summation
d) Select Columns
e) Select Report.

(Only one answer is correct)

Answer – e

Explanation:

The SAP List Viewer unifies and simplifies the use of lists in the R/3 System. A uniform user interface and list format is available for all lists. You can view subtotals and totals rows in both single level lists and multilevel sequential lists.

Features of the SAP list viewer are:

- Navigation
- Sorting
- Select List
- Select Details/Select columns
- Totaling/Summation
- Status display
- Search/Printing

Select Report is not a function of SAP List Viewer.

12) Which of the following are types of selection variables for report variants?

a) Table variables from TVARV
b) Dynamic date calculation
c) Posting period
d) Fiscal year

(Moe than one answer is correct)

Answer – a, b

Explanation:

You can use user-specific selection variables to make input values in a variant user-dependent. Table variables from TVARV and dynamic date calculation are the selection variables for report variants.

13) Identify the correct statements with respect to the lock box.

a) A lock box file contains the following information: Customer name and customer number in the SAP System, customer MICR number (bank routing number and account number), check amount, invoice number, payment date, payment amounts/deductions per invoice, and reasons for deductions.
b) A lock box is a service that banks provide to facilitate the orderly collection and processing of incoming payments
c) Banks receive the payments and create a data file from the payment advice information and payment amounts.
d) All of the above

(More than one answer is correct)

Answer – d

Explanation:

Banks receive the payments and create a data file from the payment advice information and payment amounts. The checks are then credited to your bank account. The file is sent to you at regular intervals so that you can update your books.

14) When entering a document using a foreign currency, which date is used to determine the exchange rate if the translation date is not entered?

a) Posting Date
b) Document date
c) Baseline date

d) Entry date

(Only one answer is correct)

Answer – a

Explanation:

The exchange rate is converted based on the posting date for a foreign currency document.

Solution Manager

1. Your company is implementing SAP SRM and SAP SCM in phase 1. They are planning a phase 2 to include SAP CRM and SAP BI. Their goal is to minimize changes & therefore costs. They ask you for an opinion on when to install the Solution Manager.

Choose the correct answer.

(Only one answer is correct).

a. SAP Solution manager should be implemented between Phase I and Phase II. This would ensure that resources are available.

b. SAP Solution manager should be implemented at the beginning of Phase I as it is only used for project planning & configuration via Roadmaps. If we don't implement it in phase 1 we should not implement it at all.

c. SAP Solution manager should be implement at the beginning of Phase I as it can configure to help systems via roadmaps and it is required by SAP for software maintenance of SAP SCM and the other SAP systems in our landscape.

Answer

a

Ideally, Solution Manager should be implemented at the beginning to Phase I, but in case it is required to minimize the change and hence keep costs down, it is better to implement it after Phase I, rather than not implement it at all.

Solution Manager supports the following functions across all stages of implementation.

- Implementation
    - Functional
    - Technical
    - Transactional
- Operation
    - Services
    - Solution Monitoring
    - Operations
- Supports all Project Phases
    - Project Preparation
    - Blueprint
    - Realization
    - Final Preparation
    - Go-live & Support
- Monitoring Tools
    - EWA – Early Watch Alert
    - System
    - Business Process
    - Interface

2. Excluding the Continuous improvement phase, how many phases are there in the Accelerated SAP roadmap

(Only one answer is correct).

a. 4

b. 3

c. 5

d. 6

Answer

c

The implementation of your SAP System covers the following phases:

Project Preparation

In this phase you plan your project and lay the foundations for successful implementation. It is at this stage that you make the strategic decisions crucial to your project:

Define your project goals and objectives

Clarify the scope of your implementation

Define your project schedule, budget plan, and implementation sequence

Establish the project organization and relevant committees and assign resources

Business Blueprint

In this phase you create a blueprint using the Question & Answer database (Q & A db), which documents your enterprise's requirements and establishes how your business processes and organizational structure are to be represented in the SAP System. You also refine the original project goals and objectives and revise the overall project schedule in this phase.

Realization

In this phase, you configure the requirements contained in the Business Blueprint. Baseline configuration (major scope) is followed by final configuration (remaining scope), which can consist of up to four cycles. Other key focal areas of this phase are conducting integration tests and drawing up end user documentation.

Final Preparation

In this phase you complete your preparations, including testing, end user training, system management, and cutover activities. You also need to resolve all open issues in this phase. At this stage you need to ensure that all the prerequisites for your system to go live have been fulfilled.

Go Live & Support

In this phase you move from a pre-production environment to the live system. The most important elements include setting up production support, monitoring system transactions, and optimizing overall system performance.

After your system has gone live, you can use a separate Roadmap with six work packages, in order to optimize your SAP System continuously.

3. Which of the following statements are FALSE (more than one answer may be correct)?

(More than one answer is correct)

a. New business process procedure can be created from a standard template

b. SAP Solution Manager is only used during the implementation phase of a project

c. The Knowledge Warehouse contains numerous accelerators

d. Any person can access project documentation in SAP Solution Manager

Answer

b, d

SAP Solution Manager is used not only for implementation, but also for support and ongoing operations.

Access to Solution Manager is restricted by authorizations.

4. Which of the following activities would occur in Phase 2? Select the correct answers.

(More than one answer is correct)

a. Finalizing the project scope

b. Defining and documenting all business requirements, both functional and technical

c. End user training

d. Cycle and integration testing

Answer

a, b

Phase 2 is the Business Blueprint phase.

In this phase you create a blueprint using the Question & Answer database (Q&Adb), which documents your enterprise's requirements and establishes how your business processes and organizational structure are to be represented in the SAP System. You also refine the original project goals and objectives and revise the overall project schedule in this phase.

5. Which of the following activities would occur in Phase 3? Select the correct answers.

(More than one answer is correct)

a. Configuring the system

b. Testing the system to ensure that it meets the specified business requirements

c. Developing training materials

d. End user training

e. Defining the project scope

Answer

a, b, c

Third phase is the Realization phase.

In this phase, you configure the requirements contained in the Business Blueprint. Baseline configuration (major scope) is followed by final configuration (remaining scope), which can consist of up to four cycles. Other key focal areas of this phase are conducting integration tests and drawing up end user documentation.

6. Which of the following statements are TRUE regarding SAP Solution Manager?

(More than one answer is correct)

a. It is the same toolset as ASAP

b. It is an integrated platform that controls both implementation and operation of the live system

c. Supports customers in ALL project phases, from creating a blueprint to configuring business processes and testing through support of the live environment

d. Can only be used to manage business processes on SAP

Answer

b, c

The solution manager has much more functionality than the ASAP toolset.

It is used for end to end management of solutions covering not just SAP systems but also third party application/interfaces.

7. Which of the following statements are FALSE. Select the incorrect answers.

(More than one answer is correct)

a. Only Project Managers can use SAP Solution Manager

b. Scoping is based on components rather than processes

c. Accelerators are found in the Knowledge Warehouse in SAP Solution Manager in the form of templates

d. Test cases cannot be reused

e. Documentation in SAP Solution Manager is limited to the documentation types delivered by SAP

Answer

a, b, d, e

Solution Manager can be used by anyone depending on their system authorizations levels.

Scoping is almost always based on processes rather than individual components.

Test cases are meant to be developed once and reused over and over, e.g. in the System Tests, User Acceptance Test, Stress Test, Post Go Live User Verification tests etc. And also from project to project depending on functionality deployed.